MW00437952

SCARS OF WISDOM

By Alonte' Thomas

TABLE OF CONTENTS

Introduction/Prologue:

From Atlanta, GA, Rashad, Lil John John, and Neko were a group of young friends who were leaving their teenager years and becoming men who were trying to find their way in life. They grew up in Adamsville, one of the many high poverty areas of Atlanta, based on the west side of the city. Like the average young boy or girl in the hood, the plan was to turn a penny into a dollar and a plastic spoon into a gold one. After Rashad received the call that his mother's next-door neighbors had assaulted his little sister, everyone's life changed. The group of young friends took loss after loss even after believing in God wholeheartedly, which was something that would never change and when they finally looked back on it, all the losses that they took finally made sense.

Chapter 1. *Please Don't Die On Me*

June 24th, 2013

As Rashad lies out on the front lawn of the home right across the street from his mother's house, blood leaks out of his chest like a water faucet. Luckily, his mom's neighbor, who has nursing experience, applies pressure to his chest to at least try to stop some of the blood that's coming out of his body. Since her hands are tied up as she tries to stop blood from gushing out his body, the group of friends as well as his family pleads for him to breath in order to avoid a panic attack. Jake, which is Rashad's youngest brother runs out of his mom's house with a huge pot of water preparing to throw it on his big brother thinking it will make the situation better.

"Jake, no!" yells the neighbor, "If that water gets in his bloodstream he may die!"

"Fuck! Man, I can't lose another brother to these streets they got us fucked up!" says Lil John John, Rashad's closest friend.

Silence came from Neko, his second closest friend whose mind went blank because he figured these were the final moments of watching his dawg take his last breath right in front of his eyes.

"Please don't die on me, I love you with everything in me!" says Chasity, while looking him in his eyes before he lost the energy to blink them again.

"Oh My God!" are the words that come out of his mom's mouth due to the fact the things her eyes are seeing right now are too hard for her to even imagine. The gruesome scene has her so shell-shocked that she shits on herself, literally. Not to mention she has on a sundress but from the hurt that her eyes are witnessing, having on a dress is the last thing on her mind.

"Y'all make sure he doesn't close his eyes!" yells the neighbor.

"Baby just focus on breathing, you'll be okay," is the last thing Rashad will remember before opening his eyes a week later in ICU.

Chapter 2. *Loyalty Over Royalties*
(Rewind 1 year back)

Reacting to the sound of the doorbell, Rashad opened the door to see Lil John John along with two females.

"Damn bro, y'all went to a party without me? The hell you coming from with these sexy ladies?" Rashad asked curiously.

"We coming from church nigga, every New Year's Eve at 12 you know where I'm at," said Lil John John.

This was the first time in the last three years Rashad hadn't gone to church so he felt as if Lil John John was trying to make him feel bad.

"Man, God know I love him while you tryna talk dat shit, who these lil tenders you got with you though?" Rashad asked excitedly.

"Santana & Angel. Santana my baby though, just brought the new years in with her at church, so we can start this thang off right. I brought Angel for you, see what's up wit her."

As the conversation continued between the group, Lil John John realized he left his weed at home and had nothing to smoke on. "Bro you got weed?" he asked.

"Yea, but I don't have no swishers," Rashad replied.

"Say less, I'm bout to ride to the store right quick," said Lil John John. Immediately after he left, the conversation between Rashad and the two girls began.

"So where are you from?" Santana asked.

"I'm from Atlanta, Adamsville to be exact," Rashad responded.

"Do you have any kids?" asked Angel.

"Not yet," Rashad said, "our generation is full of disloyal motherfuckas these days and I rather be single than put myself in a questionable relationship."

"That's very understandable, so do you have a girlfriend?" asked Angel.

"If I did would it matter?" he responded. Both girls reply with laughs as they keep the conversation going.

"You are kind of cute though, ever had a threesome?"

Rashad was caught completely off guard, not because he was scared or nervous, but the fact that those words didn't come from Angel, they came from Santana, the pretty girl that Lil John John was falling for.

"Naw, not yet," Rashad said replying to the question, which he's telling the truth about. There were a lot of things that he had scratched off his bucket list, but a threesome wasn't one of them. Minutes into the conversation between the trio, the topic of discussion was about nothing other than sex and being that it's no topic Rashad wasn't used to, he had yet to notice anything unusual.

Arriving in the middle of the X-rated conversation was Lil John John. Seeing him walk through the door, the conversation quickly ends.

"Well damn, why everybody get so quiet?" Lil John John asked curiously as if he already heard loud voices outside of Rashad's room before he walked in. The awkwardness caused Rashad to put on a facial expression backing up everything that Lil John John had just asked. *Why did they become so quiet all of sudden*, Rashad wondered. Something wasn't right and that was the moment Rashad realized that maybe Santana wasn't the girl Lil John John thought she was and her promiscuous ways were being exposed.

"We was talking about sex and threesomes bro, figured it was a group convo so I don't know why they got so quiet when you came in," said Rashad.

"Well let me in!" Lil John John said jokingly but yet serious at the same time while looking back and forth at both girls. In return, Santana put her head down while Angel acted as if she just received the most important text message in years. Instantly the actions taken by the girls put Lil John John in a bad vibe and being that he was the one to bring them over in the first place it was totally understandable.

"Oh okay, I see what's going on, handle ya business fool. I'm bout to step in the living room and roll this weed up," said Lil John John. The way the situation was playing out made Rashad feel uncomfortable as Lil John John did exactly what he said he was going to do, and closed the door right behind him. Rashad didn't like the fact that Santana was being devious, but he kept his cool. Some minutes go by then a text message comes though his phone and it was Lil John John.

"Bro fuck that bitch for me, so you can prove she ain't shit!"

In the back of Rashad's mind, he understands exactly where Lil John John was coming from but the possible party wasn't deep enough for Rashad to overlook the bad vibes.

"Man bring yo monkey ass in here and let's get high," Rashad said. As if nothing happened, Lil John John comes back in the room and proceeds with the smoke session. Smoking the weed until they couldn't handle it anymore, Lil John John decided to take the girls back home on a good note, being that the weed wouldn't even allow him to look back on the bad vibes that were experienced.

Chapter 3. *Expect The Unexpected*

1:30 a.m. Rashad's phone rings, it's Lil John John and they haven't spoken in about two days.

"Where you at fool?"

"I'm at grandma spot what's the move?" Rashad replied.

"I need you to come ride with me right quick, so I can serve my folks some molly."

Molly, the closest drug to ecstasy, was used in either a crystal or powder form before it enters the body and Lil John was great at selling the product. Minutes later, Lil John John pulled up to Rashad's grandmother's home where he was staying at the moment and honked the horn for Rashad to come out.

"You got your nine on you right?" asked Lil John John right after Rashad closed the passenger door to the 1998 green Ford Escort, which goes by the name of "Roxanne."

"That's like asking a dope fiend if he got a lighter nigga, what you think?" Rashad said as they both laughed at the remark while heading to their destination.

The gun Rashad had access to wasn't actually his, but he had access to it when he needed it. It was something left behind by his grandmother's husband to protect their home from any intruders. Rashad wasn't a bad person at all or a killer to say the least, but he was a product of environment, which made him protect himself at all times. The mindset came about from experience, which taught him that anything could happen at any time while being in the wrong place at the wrong time. They arrive to the destination and meet up with a young lady maybe 5'5", dark skin with braids that dropped down to her ass walking towards the driver door where Lil John John sat behind the wheel.

"Hey baby," she said as she speaks to Lil John John, it was obvious she was a familiar customer.

"Let me get 3 of em." In other words, she was asking for 3 capsules, which was what Lil John John puts his molly in to stretch the profit or to make it look like more than what it actually is. A technique any bona fide hustler would understand. Once Lil John John gave the lady what she asked for, it prompts him to become curious and ask about her night.

"Damn lil mama, it seems to me as if you bout to have a party, let me and my boy join…"

"I would but my boyfriend is in the house," she replied.

"That's cool, maybe we can get a room one day this week and handle grown folks' business," Lil John John implies.

"We most definitely can and I have a friend for your friend," she responded, trying to include Rashad in the festivities as well.

To her surprise, the conversation between the two didn't excite Rashad as much as she may have expected. Although Rashad was listening to the conversation, he's also just as busy watching his surroundings to make sure that he and Lil John John made it back safely. After all, that was Rashad's main reason for being there in the first place—making sure they arrived back to the westside, where Rashad's grandmother resides. Looking up at the sky, Rashad saw the night wasn't too far from sunrise. Opening the passenger side door of Roxanne, before getting out the car, Lil John John brought it to Rashad's attention that he needed some weed for the night. Though Lil John John and Rashad both sold weed, Lil John John's weed wasn't as strong or potent as his right-hand man's. Lil John John's marijuana was for profit purposes only and after the transaction they called it a night and parted ways.

Bang, Bang, Bang!!!! Rashad looks at his phone to see that it's 8:00 a.m. and was pissed off to hear someone banging on the door that early. Expecting to see Jehovah Witnesses, he was hit with a surprise. He opened the door to see none other than Chasity, his 5'4" redbone drama infested girlfriend of three years. Halfway asleep and confused, "Damn bay what's up? It's too early for this shit," Rashad said. He wanted to let her in, but he instantly had flashbacks of her not being able to keep her hands to herself.

"Fuck all that! I mean I been calling you all night and got no answer. You never go to sleep early so what bitch you was fucking?" Talking through the burglar bar door, he wanted to slam the wood door in her face but he knew it would only add fuel to the fire.

"Sleep," Rashad responded while his eyes are still halfway shut.

"Rashad stop fucking playing with me. I can't keep playing the fool for you and open the fucking door!" screamed Chasity.

Rashad wanted to let her in, but his mind was telling him: No. He's already suffering consequences of her jealously, which caused him to have a temporary phone since putting his recent iPhone in the washer machine along with his dirty clothes just so he couldn't use it.

"Man, I was sleep! You so busy trying not to be a fool that you gone play yourself out the situation," Rashad said as it became obvious he's becoming irritated. Before you knew it, it was an all-out argument with a burglar bar door attached with a screen separating them.

"You know what man, fuck you Rashad! I'm about to go and I hope that hoe was worth it."

"You came all the way over here just to fuck my sleep up and spill all that negative ass energy on my grandma porch?! Bitch bye!" Rashad said angrily before slamming the door to her back. Although knocking on the door this early pissed him off, there was nothing unusual because he knew firsthand that Chasity loved drama more than anything. As Rashad got back in his bed, he's hit with a surprise that he couldn't see coming a mile away. It was a direct message on Instagram from Santana, the girl Lil John John brought over a few days ago.

Chapter 4. *Fuck Love*

The devil was working early that morning and Rashad couldn't deny it, from his girlfriend popping up early in the morning talking that bullshit, to his closest friend's companion sending him disturbing messages.

"Hey Rashad, it's Santana from the other day. So, what's up with the conversation my friend and I were having with you on New Year's?" Rashad read the message but didn't reply. The way Instagram direct messages were set up, once you read someone's message it showed them their message had been read. As though that wasn't enough for her to realize that he wasn't interested, she sent another message asking for his number. Rashad had never been known as the gossiping type, but he was a strong believer in loyalty from every angle. Confused by her actions Rashad had to check in with Lil John John to see if they were actually dating or not. The phone was ringing and Lil John John answered, "Sup foo tell me some good?"

"As long as I see it no complaints... Say bro what's up with you and Santana though? Y'all really rocking or that's just something to do?" Rashad asked.

"Hell yea bro them my people, she was just crying on my shoulder last night telling me about her family issues or what not. What just made you call and ask that?" Lil John John asked curiously.

He had just said it all and that was the moment Rashad came up with the conclusion that Santana wasn't shit.

"Well she on Instagram still talking about a threesome and asking for my number. I just feel as if it was genuine, she would've asked you for my number. I'm not with all that gossiping shit, but we done been down this road before and you always kept me on my toes so I got to do the same for you."

Lil John John earned Rashad's trust and loyalty years ago when Rashad's girlfriend Chasity approached Lil John John in a sneaky way hoping it wouldn't get back to Rashad. Little did she know, Lil John John kept Rashad on his toes about everything. With that being said, it still wasn't enough for Rashad's love for Chasity to die.

"Damn man I was feeling shawty too! Man, these hoes ain't shit. Crying to me bout her problems and shit, ol' stanking ass bish!"

It was obvious Lil John John was feeling some type of way. Regardless of his emotions, he remained to treat the situation like a natural born playa and didn't say a word to her about it but rather changed his actions and vibes toward her. Rashad somewhat felt bad because he felt if the two of them clashed he would ultimately be the reason they went downhill, but who gives a fuck? It's always loyalty over royalty let Rashad tell it. It's a lot of dudes fucking on their friend's girlfriend in Atlanta, while allowing the relationship to portray fake love but that wasn't the circle Rashad wanted to be in. He treated his friends how he wanted to be treated and as the saying goes "actions speak louder than words."

Chapter 5. *Hard Head Make A Soft Ass*

The antidote to the struggle is hustle! That was Rashad's motto and he lived by it. He was born into a family of hustlers, mom was the only one to graduate out of his immediate family before he was able to, dad dropped out in middle school, and each of his uncles dropped out in high school. Guess you can say that they weren't the best role models for him but if there's one thing he was taught it was how to get some money and stand strong on his own two feet. Rashad went to Benjamin E. Mays High School located in Adamsville, which at the time he resided in "Allen Temple," an apartment complex located off Martin Luther King Drive. Most people would call it "The Hood" but Rashad called it home.

Attending Mays High before getting kicked out he left behind his posse that goes by the name, "Da Crew." Rashad, Neko, Lil John John, Richie, White boy John, and Blake all formed the posse. They also all attended Mays at some point in time. Rashad and Neko both reside in Allen Temple so they usually kicked it with each other on a regular day basis. The two of them basically did everything together—ran trains on a couple girls, finessed a few dudes out of money, worked at the same summer jobs and even went through similar hardships. They were also gambling addicts when it came to the dice, from craps, high dice, to even cee-lo and could probably smoke Snoop Dogg to sleep on his best day. Speaking of gambling, that's exactly where they met, in the hallway of the apartment building at the dice game in Allen Temple, while they were both in the tenth grade. Neko was trying to scrape up every dollar he could because he had a set of beautiful twin daughters on the way. Yes, he started young but if you asked him does he regret it, the answer would be never.

Lil John John and White Boy John were both known for their goofiness and ability to make the angriest person in the room laugh. White Boy John got his name to distinguish the two being that both their names are John. He's a light skin pretty boy, with curly hair that couldn't stay braided if he tried but he wasn't white. Richie, the silent assassin and also the founder of "Da Crew." He was known for his charming ways, making music and having financial income due to the fact that his mother passed away some years back, which put him in a position to receive a check every month because of it. Being 1 out of 2 of the friends to have a vehicle was also a plus. You could say he really had it going on, but once you lose your mom who knows what's on mind, of course there's pain you may not show.

Blake was the tall, skinny, lanky friend who you would mistake for having broomsticks hooked up to his hips from the view of his long skinny legs. He had a heart of gold and was a strong believer in Black Power and anything concerning the black community in an uplifting and positive way. Blake's also a huge Louis Farrakhan fan, which influenced him to become Muslim as well as a black nationalist. Rashad was the first out Da Crew to get kicked out of Mays High permanently for shooting dice in the hallway during class. Weeks later, Lil John John was right behind him for getting caught with a few grams of marijuana on school property. Although they left on two separate occasions, they both ended up leaving the rest of Da Crew behind at Mays high school. Since they all stay on the westside of Atlanta, there wasn't a big difference in how much they saw each other being that they weren't attending the same school anymore. The result of Lil John John and Rashad getting kicked out of Mays High forced them to enroll into alternative school, which was the only school in Atlanta that would accept them.

Alonzo A. Crim Open Campus, the jungle mixed with every savage that's been kicked out of their original high school in the city of Atlanta filled with lions, monkey niggas, and bears. The females were professional boosters. If they weren't skipping school stealing high-end clothing from the mall, they were at school doing hair for whoever had the money to get it done. The school even had a daycare for the students who had kids and it was free! Being that Rashad and Lil John John got kicked out of their original school already, you would have thought they learned their lesson but like mama says, "A hard head always make a soft ass and you gone learn boy!" Words that always went in one ear and out the other.

They couldn't win for losing and Rashad could remember it like yesterday… A group of young teenagers including Rashad and Lil John John were in the upstairs restroom gambling, playing craps with a set of white dice.

"Nobody Move!" screamed the sloppy body principal bursting through the bathroom door with one policeman standing behind him. Apparently, he heard the dice bouncing off the floor onto the wall. It was a nice size restroom made with numerous stalls, so it was not easy to point out who's all in the restroom at once. Immediately after hearing the principal's voice, Rashad ran into a restroom stall hoping he could get out of the scenario by claiming his only reason for being in the restroom was to urinate. Lil John, on the other hand, opened the restroom window and attempted to escape by jumping on the roof of the school, while running around like a chicken with his head cut off just to end up right back in the same exact window he figured he escaped from. Some may say that Lil John John went overboard, but when you already have a record for getting kicked out of school and a mother that's sick of your shit, you may tend to do whatever it takes to escape trouble as well. Although Lil John John tried his best to escape another troubling situation, it still wasn't enough and minutes later they found themselves right back in the principal's office facing permanent suspension.

In a different school but keeping their same ways forced them to blame no one but themselves and Mr. Jackson, the principal of Crim High School was quite tired of seeing the two in the mist of everything.

"Well Mr. Thomas, we've given you chance after chance, now I have to make an example out of you or everyone else is going to think I'm something to play with."

"Noooo," says Rashad with a smirk on his face. "Mr. Jackson I was just using the restroom to take a piss! You can't blame me for having to urine at the wrong time!" Rashad responded.

"Whatever you have to say keep it, because you knew that they were shooting dice, so common sense should have told you to go use a different restroom knowing you've been walking on thin ice lately," said Mr. Jackson.

As the principal expressed his thoughts, he calmly wrote a description of the incident on a piece of paper and by that moment Rashad had knew that his ass was grass. The next step for Mr. Jackson was to contact his mother. Rashad's mom usually flew to his rescue, but she was tired of breaking her back for her hardheaded ass son (in her words). That's half the reason why she kicked Rashad out of the house at fourteen and the other half was because she assumed Rashad smoked weed around his younger brother Jake while babysitting. Although she was wrong about her son smoking in front of his little brother, the marijuana smell on Rashad's fingertips and breath made her feel as if her point was proven.

"I'm sorry to inform you Mr. Thomas, but I'm going to suspend you for the remaining of the year, you're not allowed back on the premises until next school year," said Mr. Jackson.

"Man that's bullshit!" yelled Rashad, "How you gone blame me for somebody else actions when I was just taking a piss!?"

Mr. Jackson sat in silence while looking Rashad directly in his eyes as if he'd said everything that he possibly had to say and was done talking.

Rashad supposed to be in the 12th grade alongside Lil John John but due to getting kicked out of school numerous times, he was still one grade level below, which made him class of 2011'. Stuck in the principal's office, all attention was now on Lil John John. Of course, Rashad was expecting him to get the worse end of the stick being that he tried to escape on the roof, but boy was he wrong. Lil John John was about to graduate in three months, not to mention his mom worked for the Atlanta Public School System, so to everyone's surprise Mr. Jackson spared him. Rashad was highly upset about it, but he respected it. True enough, Lil John John was only three months away from graduating and Rashad wanted that blessing for him as much as he wanted it for himself. Plus, he was starting to become Rashad's right-hand man, so he couldn't direct any of the anger he was feeling towards him. Lil John John graduated a few months later and proved a lot of haters wrong, even some of his own family. Coming from poverty, he had a hand few of believers and a pool full of doubters but eventually they all became believers.

The next following school year for Rashad was the best of each of his high school years because he had less neighborhood friends with him as well as distractions all around. The change happened to be a good thing for him because it allowed him to focus more on his schoolwork and watching his friends leave him behind gave him all the motivation he needed. Though Rashad and Lil John John were always in some shit, they were highly intelligent and sophisticated—meaning book smart and street smart—so it wasn't hard for neither of the two to pass a class with flying colors if they really put their mind to it. The bigger issue was just getting them to show up to class. Rashad eventually graduated that following year and made his family extremely proud. Especially his father being that he was a middle school dropout. So proud to be a graduate, thinking about all the troubles he came across, Rashad was sure that college wasn't for him. With those types of thoughts maneuvering through his mind it was clear that he had yet to learn life.

Chapter 6. *Leave With More Than What You Came With*

Awakened out of his daydream by his loud metro cellular phone, Rashad saw it was Neko and he was calling to make sure Rashad was home before catching a ride from Allen Temple. That's when Rashad realized he had dozed off while reminiscing on his old high school days.

"Nephew come empty my bag!" It was the voice of Rashad's uncle Kennyman telling him to come empty his urine bag. Apparently Kennyman heard Rashad talking on the phone and thought that was the perfect time to grasp his attention. Kennyman was 45, paralyzed neck down, and had been that way since the age of 23. He was in a bad car accident, which broke his neck. Although he was not able to walk, he could never be underestimated because he's liable to do more than the eye can see.

Rashad and his uncle Kennyman had a very close relationship with one another and ever since Rashad's mother kicked him out at 14, he had been staying with both his grandma Betty and uncle Kennyman ever since. His dad was in the streets at an early age and wasn't around as much as Rashad wanted at times, but that never stopped him from being a great support system, which caused Rashad to love and respect his father genuinely. Being that Rashad's dad and his uncle Kennyman were cut from similar cloths, it was easier for Rashad to listen to his uncle than it would be from someone who didn't have anything going for themselves trying to give him advice.

"Nephew who that is at the door?" asked Kennyman as Rashad emptied out his bag into his urine cup. Having a hood on, neither Kennyman nor Rashad could see the face. There was a camera on each corner of his Grandma Betty's home and with the camera boxes being set up in

Kennyman's room, he saw everything first. Grandma Betty was physically assaulted in a home invasion earlier in her life, in which the home invaders tied her up with rope hoping to find money. Guess you could say, Rashad's family had been through trials and tribulation over time but through it all they still thanked Jesus everyday simply because they could.

Rashad opened the door to see none other than gambling ass Neko and before he could even open the screen door, "Boy guess what happen last night! Man, I done hit Big Tum on the dice for 1,000 last night!"

"Sound like you handled yo business then nigga" Rashad replied.

"Naw man I fucked around got greedy and lost the whole bankroll right back to him!"

Rashad couldn't believe his ears. "Man, no fuck you didn't do no retarded shit like that, you posed to at least left with 500 bro!"

"Yea I know, I tripped out. You know how it be when you lose a lil money then become determined to get back what you lost, just to realize you right back where you started? At that, I've witnessed you go out bad plenty times on the dice so don't be tryna lecture me!"

Rashad replied in laughter knowing he couldn't argue because he knew Neko was right, plus he'd been in that same seat Neko was in at that moment once before. That's a part of gambling—sometimes you win, sometimes you lose, but the best teacher of it all was the experience. Experience being the #1 teacher in Rashad's life taught him that if you go up big on any type of gamble whether it's cards, dice, or even betting on shots in basketball, you have to leave with more than you came with. It's a must but like the old saying goes, "Every dog has his day," and Neko just had his.

While breaking down a swisher sweet to stuff with some good kush to ease Neko's mind from his nightmare, comes a knock at the front door. It's Lil John John and he was just stopping by to vibe for a minute.

"Damn bro, a nigga can push up on Rashad but won't even come my way period... Niggas act like I'm in a whole different city or some," Neko said.

"Ha Ha Ha boy shut yo black crayon body having ass up... just been tryna get some money," Lil John John replied.

"Speaking of money let me tell you how this fool lost the money!" screamed Rashad. As Rashad explained Neko's nightmare as if he were right there to witness it, Neko cut him off as if he was tired of hearing about it.

"Yea yea fuck all that! Seems like ain seen y'all niggas in forever, let's hit the city tonight," Neko insisted.

"That freak bitch diamond did tell me Club Bankhead supposed to be loaded tonight we can slide through," Rashad said.

"That's the move then. I just came through to see what's going on over here. I'm bout to pull up at Gwop Studio to make a couple tracks," said Lil John John.

Gwop is a music engineer/producer from the up north area that has his own studio built inside his home. He moved to Atlanta to make a name for himself in the music industry and is doing a damn good job. Gwop has worked with major labels such as BadBoy, Def Jam, artist such as P.Diddy and Young Thug as well. He also showed a lot of genuine love to "Da Crew" overtime and was greatly appreciated.

"I'm gone bro I'll call you bout 11:30-12 to see if y'all ready," said Lil John John as he walks out the door.

"I think I'm gone kick it over here till we dip later on cause if I go back to the partments I'm bound to touch some dice and I don't need to be nowhere near those," said Neko.

"Mama always said a hard head gone make a soft ass!" said Rashad. The comment made Neko laugh so hard he coughed up every piece of smoke he had just inhaled, burning his throat.

"It's all good dawg. We win some, we lose some, you'll catch his ass slipping one of these days," encouraging words spoken by Rashad. If the people around you don't speak encouragement upon you, then what's the reason for them being around?

Chapter 7. *This Isn't My First Rodeo*

"Man wake yo big nose ass up! Lil John John say he on the way…" the voice of Neko runs through Rashad's ear but he doesn't budge while he's lying on the sofa in his living room.

"Bro get yo parrot nose having ass up!"

Trying the second time, he finally gets up laughing as if the parrot nose joke was actually funny. Rashad was an attractive young fellow who never really had problems with the ladies but that nose however was like a bell pepper on his face and Uncle Kennyman along with his friends wasted no time joking about it daily. Rashad looked at his phone to see thirty missed calls and eight text messages. Sure enough, 27 out of the 30 calls were Chasity and she's more than positive that he was somewhere getting his dick sucked. The other few missed calls were from diamond, the big booty stallion that he was supposed to meet at the club. Rashad had just landed off cloud nine from the several blunts of Kush that he and Neko had smoked and he was too calm to argue with Chasity. True enough, he missed her. It was evident Chasity needed some sexual healing and Rashad knew it. A simple text "I was sleep, and I'm bout to go to the club. I'm coming to get you when I leave" was all it took. Their relationship was strange to say the least, but they really thought they were in love.

Rashad wasn't really the club type and if you asked him why, his response was "cause niggas don't know how to act" every time. On the other hand, Neko wanted some city love for the night so Da Crew was down for the ride. Before they knew it, the time was 1:25 a.m. and you could hear the horn of Mrs. Whitfield's dark red PT cruiser outside. Mrs. Whitfield was Lil

John John's mom and to say she's a character would be an understatement. It's just something about the women with the first name "Betty" that caused everyone to love them and she loved Lil John John twice as much.

As Rashad and Neko walked up to the dark red PT cruiser all they heard was…

"ALL MY NIGGAS THEY KEEP IT PLAYA! PLAYAAA… I'M RUNNING THIS SHIT JUST LIKE THE MAYOR! MAYORRR…!"

It was new music that Lil John John & 4'z Up Quintez had just created. Lil John John's rap name was "Young Fly" and very underrated lyrically or not taking serious enough because he was always looked at as a joke teller. 4'z Up Quintez had been pursuing his rap career ever since a young age as well but hasn't caught his break yet. The two of them made great music together and from the sounds of their music you would've thought they were already signed to a record label, but they weren't. The duo was a perfect case of great talent just waiting to get heard by the right person. Lil John John's grind was so mean that he performed shows in khakis from Wal-Mart with Nike flip-flops because in reality that was all he had to wear. He was a product of environment all the way around and was actually a huge influence on Rashad's life whether he knew it or not.

Club Bankhead was directly in the hood right off Bankhead Highway. You probably heard T.I., Shawty Lo, Outkast and many other artists express their love for Bankhead on numerous hit songs being that it's a familiar part of the westside. It's also the home of upcoming artists and hustlers that you may never hear about it. Although it said highway, Bankhead is just actually a very long road, so long that you could ride the street all the way to Alabama no cuts or turns, straight shot. Da Crew hadn't even made it to the front of the club before they realized that it wasn't an ordinary night. What gave them that impression was the cars parked a half-mile from the club.

"Damn Bankhead Lit tonight!" said Neko as he expressed his excitement.

"No way we parkin all the way back here though," Rashad implied.

"Hell naw foo, I got my pocket rocket on me anyway so we need to be right in front of the door," Lil John John replied. Pocket rocket was another word for a small gun that could fit in your pocket, shoe, or boots for no one to notice. Obviously it was small enough to sneak in the club but that wasn't Lil John John's intention. Lil John John just wanted to state the fact that he had his gun in the car to avoid car break-ins. Driving towards the front of the club to their surprise, there was a parking space calling their name as if someone had just pulled off.

"Where you at?" a text comes through Rashad's phone from Diamond right when the PT cruiser was put in park, talk about perfect timing.

"I'm coming through the door," texted Rashad.

"I'm right by the bar," she replied

Big booty Diamond... She wasn't fat but wasn't skinny. Kinda reminded you of the redbone porn star who goes by the name "Pinky." Short and thick as the grocery store the day food stamps hit the EBT card. As Da Crew walked through the door, Neko sparked up the blunt of weed he pre-rolled in the PT cruiser as they found an area not too crowded by the pool tables. Immediately after they found their spot in the club, Rashad went searching for the biggest booty at the bar. In the meantime, Lil John John split 2 swisher sweets down the middle, preparing to roll and 'extendo', 2 or more swisher sweets connected together to form a flute look-a-alike made of weed. Quite wonderful experience let Lil John John tell it.

Rashad finally spots Diamond and once in her reach after making eye contact, she grabbed his dick as if it was playdoh or some type of stress balls in her hands. Luckily, she was gentle.

"So what's up with you? When you gone throw that ass back?" Rashad asked.

"Boy this pussy gone fuck your mind up that's why you haven't got it yet. I'm doing you a favor," she replied.

From the smell of her breath, she was already tipsy and of course someone probably treated her to drinks before Rashad arrived, but he could care less.

"Naw, you probably been holding on to that lil pussy cause it stank… You can keep all that game for a lame," Rashad said.

She burst out in laughter, which forced him to laugh with her, and from the vibe he could tell that it was going to be a good night. While not wanting to spend all his time in the club flirting, Rashad cut the convo short and walked back to the area where his friends were.

"Here you go foo."

It was Lil John John passing Rashad the flute look-a-like extendo. Being that it's dark inside Club Bankhead with flashing disco lights, Rashad noticed some familiar faces but twice as many unfamiliar. An example was the light skin dude maybe 5'5 walking around with his hood on making it hard to see his face and he'd been watching the three ever since they walked in the club. It was 2:50 a.m. and the club closes at three so the party was moving to the parking lot. Walking towards the exit, Da Crew blended in with the crowd and out of nowhere someone grabs Rashad's butt. He immediately turned around in defense mode preparing to cause mayhem but it turned out to be Diamond, the big booty friend from the bar.

"Girl, I was seconds away from handling you like a man, you can't be doing that!" Rashad said.

"Boy shut yo ass up… I don't be doing all that when you slapping on my ass," Diamond said.

"You're a female, that big ol' booty supposed to be played with," explained Rashad. To read between the lines it was obvious that she intended on leaving with Rashad for the night. As the group of 4 walked out the exit doors to search for the dark red PT Cruiser, you couldn't help but notice how thick the parking lot was. It was déjà vu of a high school reunion and the moment to make contact with friends that they hadn't seen in a while. Once they exchange words with old faces they all hopped in the car to leave. They drove towards the exit of the parking lot, but seconds before taking a right onto the main road the PT cruiser was hit with a heavy object that had to be thrown. Lil John John immediately hopped out the driver seat with Rashad following suit, while Neko and Diamond both remained seated in the car. They figured it was a brick or some type of concrete, but they couldn't tell specifically because it was too many objects to distinguish from on the ground that it could have been.

"These niggas got me fucked up!" yelled Lil John John as he looked into the crowd holding his chrome 25 Caliber pistol behind his back.

"Keep that thang low bro, I don't see 12 but they are out here somewhere," Rashad said as he pleaded for Lil John John to be cautious as he was holding the gun. They're looking in the crowd, which the object came from, and noticed all eyes were on them. They stared at the crowd for a good 30 seconds before Keisha, a mutual high school friend walked out of the crowd towards the two friends.

"I love y'all boys. Y'all go home and be safe," she said.

Rashad felt as if she was trying to save them from something just as well as knowing who threw the object and it felt weird. It also felt like undercover hate at the same time. It was an awkward moment and made Lil John John want to shoot into the crowd. That was before he realized the flashing lights of the police car trying to clear out the parking lot as if they hadn't seen anything that transpired a few minutes ago.

Forced to go home, Da Crew headed back to Adamsville and was clueless to what just happened. 5 or 6 minutes into the ride from the club and...

POW! POW! POW! POW!

It was gunshots, someone was shooting at the PT Cruiser. Lil John John sold molly and weed, Rashad sold weed, and Neko didn't sell anything. Neko was better known for fucking pretty girls who have boyfriends as well as being nice with the dice regardless of the loss he took yesterday. Neither were robbers nor were they doing grimy shit in the streets. Although they sold drugs it was just enough money to keep them above water so once again they were clueless as to what's happening or maybe it was Diamond, the girl. It was hard to point the finger at her because no one knew for sure. Rashad looked into the rearview mirror to see the truck getting closer and closer.

"Man, who the fuck these niggas is!?" yelled Rashad.

POW!

Lil John John shoots 1 bullet from his 25. caliber pistol just to shoot through the back window of his mom's PT Cruiser, missing Neko's head by inches. He didn't shoot the whole window out, but he shattered it.

"Give me the fye bro! You can't drive and shoot behind you at the same time!" yelled Rashad.

"Nigga I got this! This ain't my first rodeo!" Lil John John replied.

The moment escalated quickly and got very intense fast. *POW! POW!* The black truck sent two more shots.

"Bro give me that fye! Rashad said aggressively.

"Man ain got none but three bullets, well two now since I just used one! I'm tryna wait till they ass get close so I can use em wisely!" said Lil John John.

"Well keep running the lights then, fuck it!" Rashad said.

The back seat was so quiet you would have thought Rashad and Lil John John was riding alone. After running three to four red lights, Rashad noticed that the black truck was gone.

"First thing you gone do is take this bitch home," Rashad said.

Diamond was so scared she couldn't even say anything back and the fact still remained that no one knew if she had something to do with what just took place or not. One thing for sure, Rashad knew he wasn't in the mood for sex anymore. Luckily, they all stayed in same area so there was no need to back track. First stop was Diamond, next stop was Neko's house, and the last stop was Rashad's grandmother's house.

"Be careful bro and call me when you get home," was what Rashad told Lil John John as he got out the car. It was a hell of a night but they were a product of environment, so it was nothing that would break them. Before unlocking the burglar bar door to walk into the house, a text message came through Rashad's phone. It was Chasity and out of all the words he didn't read, the ones that stood out were "and I hope you catch aids bitch!" After the night he had just been through, that shit Chasity was talking was the last thing he could care about. Then again, Rashad was the one that told her to be ready after he left club so who's really to blame?

Chapter 8. *Another Night In Atlanta*

Later that morning once Rashad woke up out of his sleep, the first thing on his mind was to never be put in that situation again while not being able to defend himself. Of course he had access to fire arms but he couldn't claim them as his own and there was nothing more that he wanted than his own. He could have went to Allen Temple where the blood gang members were, his grandmother's husband who can't stay out the streets to save his life, or even his cousins' who have a trap house right down the street from where Club Bankhead is located in 6th ward. Gathering all of his thoughts, he decided to keep it in the family and head to 6th ward. Rashad felt as if his family were a better fit knowing that any gun sold on the street could come with crime, murder, etc., and he genuinely felt as if his family wouldn't put him in a situation as such. Of course, Rashad understood that majority of the guns sold on the street were stolen but he didn't have enough money to walk into a gun store and purchase one in his government name, plus he wasn't even 21 yet.

Rashad hated asking his grandma for the keys to her silver 2000 Ford Taurus but he had no choice. Being that Chasity flattened all 4 tires and bust the windshield window of his 1999 Navy Blue Buick Regal a few months back, he was out of options.

"Hello?" Grandma Betty answered with a sleepy voice as if she was awoken out of sleep.

"Grandma I need to use your car to go to the store right quick," the same lie he used every time.

"Well come get my keys. Put them emergency brakes on and lock them doors!" He hoped out the bed, went upstairs to grab the keys, and headed toward the 6th ward neighborhood. With $100 to spend, Rashad's first gun ever purchased was a Smith &Wesson chrome 38 special revolver with shiny maple wood on the grip of the handle. It wasn't the specific gun that Rashad asked for but was the only gun his cousin had to sell. A revolver is a gun particularly made for murders because it holds all shells inside the barrel once a bullet is released, which makes it hard for policeman or homicide investigators to recover evidence. Walking out of the house from making the purchase of his first firearm, the last words Rashad heard were, "lil cuz I don't know what you got going on, but we gone pull up and lay some shit down but ya," said his cousin boo.

"Yea I know it cuz, it ain't no issues I just can't keep walking round here naked," Rashad replied as if he didn't even want his cousins to know about last night. Rashad knew his family was crazy and had no problem committing a murder if it came to it, which was all the more reason he didn't call his family for his altercations because he understood that things could go from 0 to 100 real quick.

Now that Rashad had accomplished his main goal for today it was now time to go pick up his girlfriend to make up for all the broken promises. Even though Chasity cursed Rashad out last night due to being in her feelings, he knew that if he asked her to jump she would reply, "how high?" He called her to let her know he's on the way. As if she forgot about the rude text from last night, she replied with "OK." Minutes away from Chasity mother's home, Rashad looked down to his lap where his phone was ringing while he's driving and it's the last person he wanted it to be, big booty Diamond. He doesn't answer so she sends a text. "Where you at? My pussy still wet from last night." Rashad was not even interested a little bit. For one, he's minutes away from arriving in front of Chasity mom's house. For two, he had yet to figure out if she was the reason they were followed and shot at the night before. Even if she wasn't, she was at the wrong place at the wrong time so she was dead in Rashad's eyes.

Arriving to Chasity home, Rashad honked the horn for her to come out. While he waited, he asked himself should he delete everything out his phone that would disrespect his girlfriend because she happened to be very slick with the passcodes on his phones. Rather being safe than sorry he chose to leave everything as it was. He should've learned from past experiences to delete everything out your phone when your girl comes around but for some reason he decided to go with the flow, but Neko should've already showed him to never go with the flow. A hard head gone always make a soft ass.

The passenger door of Grandma Betty's silver 2000 Ford Taurus opened and there goes the light-skinned devil that Rashad just couldn't get enough of, Chasity.

"I know you was with one of them nasty hoes last night but it's cool I'm not trippen," said Chasity while looking out the passenger window.

For her to be his girlfriend but always add "it's cool I'm not trippen," after accusing him made Rashad not trust her, not to mention some of the things he had caught her doing with his own eyes. Although he wanted a faithful relationship, a lot of her actions, ways, lies, as well as the people she hung around made Rashad the man he is today. Rashad had been with numerous of women, even some married ones but he'd never been in love with any like he loved Chasity. He wasn't perfect and would admit that and although he knew she wasn't 100% loyal, he still chose to believe in her like she was.

Backing up in the driveway of his Grandma Betty's home, he reminded Chasity that his windshield was still shattered and tires were still flat as if she didn't already know. Rashad had his mind made up that he wouldn't spend a dime on the expenses of his car from the damage that was caused by her.

"I'll fix it. Even though you was in the wrong, I had no business fucking with your car but you should have let me in the house."

The damage done to Rashad's 1999 Navy Blue Buick Regal came from not letting Chasity inside his grandmother's home assuming it was another female inside. Chasity arrived beating on windows, banging on the burglar bar door like the police, and screaming so loud that the neighbors probably heard her clearly. Despite the fact that no girl was inside with Rashad he neglected to let Chasity in. The reason for doing so was because Chasity didn't know how to keep her hands to herself once her temper was boiling. With that being said, he decided to talk to her with the burglar bar separating them, which only made it worse. She left, came back with a friend, and began to have a tag team match on his Buick Regal just to get Rashad to come out the house. Although he could have stopped her and her friend while watching them on camera in his uncle's room, he stood and watched as they took his car through demolition, which he later regretted. After a few bashes to the front windshield with a brick, enough was enough and Rashad eventually had to run outside to handle both Chasity and her friend, which was all she wanted anyway.

Snapping out of his daydream about his Buick Regal, he got out of his Grandma Betty's silver Ford Taurus followed by Chasity. Immediately after closing the house door behind them, "let me smell your dick. We haven't fucked in two or three days and I know how I left it," Chasity said unhesitatingly as if there's no such thing as a shower. Rashad wasn't caught off guard by her demand because it was no limits to how X-rated the two could get behind closed doors. In a short matter of time, she was giving Rashad the best oral sex imaginable followed by long strokes that put them both to sleep.

"Nephew...! Nephew...!" A few hours of sleep and Rashad is awaken by the voice of his uncle Kennyman. "Nephew come empty my bag!" Though the voice woke up Rashad, Chasity remained asleep, at least that's what Rashad thought. Kennyman didn't have a personal at home nurse for his paralyzed situation but his family was big enough to take up the slack. If Grandma Betty, which was his mother didn't cater to him when Rashad wasn't home they would call one of the many cousins to come over and help out, which they would usually do with no problem. While Rashad emptied his Uncle's urine bag a conversation concerning last night occurred.

"Nephew how the club was last night?" "The club was cool unk, it was the bullshit after that threw me off," said Rashad.

"Why you say that? The fuck happen?" Kennyman asked.

"Shid unk I can't even tell you, that is what's so crazy about it. We were vibing in the club, kicking our shit, and everything was cool. I be damn a few minutes after we leave out the parking lot some niggas get to shooting at our ass."

"Shooting?" Kennyman ask looking confused.

"Hell yea unk and I still don't understand that shit. Ain beefing with nobody, haven't been on no snake shit, plus lil John John and Neko be on the same shit I'm on."

Rashad didn't even speak about Diamond, the only female that was in the car with them because he had a feeling that's exactly who Kennyman was going to point the finger towards.

"Nobody had the pistol"? Uncle Kennyman asked.

"Yea Lil Jon John had his lil 25 on him but he ain't have none but three bullets."

"Three bullets?! Ahahahaha," Uncle Kennyman started to laugh as if Mike Epps the comedian had just told a joke. When Rashad thought back on the night before, he had to admit that it was kind of funny. However, when bullets are flying towards you and your adrenaline was rushing to the top, at that very moment the feeling going through your body was everything but funny. Walking around with three bullets may sound funny but truthfully, all it takes is just 1 bullet to kill someone.

"Naw for real though nephew, y'all need to be careful in these streets. I know your face card good but that don't mean shit if you at the wrong place at the wrong time," said Kennyman.

"Yea unk you right about that one, it's gone be a minute before I go back to Club Bankhead though," was how the convo between the two ended before Rashad left his Uncle's room. Just as Rashad entered his room he noticed that Chasity was wide-awake with his phone in her hand. "So, who is Diamond? And what the fuck she mean her pussy still wet from last night? You telling me that you put me on hold for one of them bitches at club Bankhead?" Chasity asked furiously.

"Hell naw bay Neko was using my…." *FOW!!!!!!!!!!!* She had just slapped the shit out Rashad before he could even get it out, followed by some punches and kicks, at least she tried to punch and kick. Though she afflicted no real pain upon Rashad, that didn't stop her from trying. Just that fast, the vibe went from 0 to 100 from love to hate. Rashad tried to calm her down, but it only gets worse.

"Fuck nigga let me go! I knew you was somewhere fucking off last night and you got me fucked up!"

She walked outside of the house where one of her friends was already waiting. Obviously, she had already called her a ride while Rashad was talking to his uncle. The relationship involving the two had more drama than the soap opera shows. Nevertheless, Rashad was sick of it and it was written all on his face. He knew he wasn't 100% loyal in the relationship just as he knew that Chasity was no better, regardless of her acting as if she was. Going back and forth with his girl about Diamond made Rashad feel crazy. He didn't even have sex with the girl that he and Chasity were both arguing about, so it made him feel like he should have fucked her since he's being treated as if he already did so. He realized it would be a while before he'd see Chasity again or even talk to her for that matter. Though he acted like he didn't care, deep inside he knew that he couldn't last long without her.

Chapter 9. *Family First*

It was a cloudy day in Atlanta, Rashad was chilling in Allen Temple with a few friends and it's been a week in a half since he'd heard from Chasity. Rashad didn't attempt to call her phone because he felt that it would only make things worse but often found himself thinking about her at least half of the day ever since. He can't help but wonder if she's somewhere bent over getting penetrated as she tries to get her mind off him. It's fucked up that he had such thoughts about his girlfriend of two years but he was no stranger to how treacherous females can be. Rashad's phone vibrates as he realizes Lil John John was calling and when he answered he immediately knew something was wrong.

"Bro… This nigga just put the choppa in my face!"

"What the hell you talking bout?" Rashad asked.

"That nigga Tommy who we went to school with. You know he got a trap in my neighborhood or whatever so I slide through to get a ounce of weed. The very next day he called me over to check on this new pack he got but it was really a set up. Someone broke in his spot the same day I got some weed so he think I had something to do with it," said Lil John John.

"So what you wanna do?" Rashad asked.

"You know what I wanna do, but I grew up with this nigga tho, true enough I fuck wit em. I just don't understand why he think I'll do him like that. The streets changing man, ain't no love out here no more or maybe it wasn't no love from the jump," said Lil John John.

"Man fuck that! Ain got the AK on me, but I got access to one! We can pull up on the block and air some shit out right now!" Rashad replied.

"Naw bro I got to get to the bottom of this shit first. I just wanted to tell you because they know who I be with so if you see em in public, watch that nigga," said Lil John John.

"Man, fuck them niggas! Where you at now? I'm in the temp tryna make some money to pay my cell phone bill but ain't shit going on. Come get me."

Not long after the convo did Lil John John arrive in his green 1996 Ford Escort known as "Roxanne" bought by his mom two years ago. Rashad hopped in and the two of them headed over to his Grandma Betty's home. Now that they'd arrived it was not much to do but get high, wait on the rain to stop pouring down, and talk about the incident that had just transpired concerning Lil John John. Before Rashad realized it, Lil John John was on his bedroom floor sleep.

"Nephew, open the door! It's ya daddy."

Opening the door to let his dad in, he got a call from his mom but didn't answer. He was not ignoring her on purpose, but the conversation Rashad and his dad were having had all his attention at the moment. They were talking about the Atlanta Falcons football team and how the quarterback, Matt Ryan, was making it hard for them to win games. His mother had called 5 times and he had yet to notice. On the 6th call Rashad realized the incoming calls and finally picked up the phone.

"What's up, Ma?"

"Rashad, your sister just got into a fight. She was fighting our neighbor's daughter when her brother jumped in and jumped on her! I need you to come see what's going on."

He didn't need to hear anything else in order to give him a reason to be on his way. Rashad hated his mom's side of town, Clayton County, the south side, but he couldn't let that stop him from going to check on his little sister. Maybe he hated it because that's where he got shot in the leg at thirteen, or maybe he hated it because his childhood love had sex with a couple people he considered his friends right after being kicked out of the house by his mom. When he attended middle school in Clayton County, he had the most disciplinary forms out of every student enrolled including all of the sixth, seventh, and eighth graders. Rashad had numerous reasons for why he hated Clayton County but neither of those reasons were going to stop him from going to check on his baby sister. "Bro get up," said Rashad as he tried to wake Lil John John up out of his sleep, but he wouldn't budge.

"Bro!" said Rashad as he tries for a second time.

"Man what's up!?" asked Lil John John as he looked at Rashad with a grumpy face.

"I need ya bro, Mom's just called talking bout somebody done jumped on my lil sister. I might need a ride to go check on her," said Rashad.

"Shid bro let's do it, but we can't drive Roxanne, she been running hot on me and we might not make it" Lil John John replied.

Rashad didn't want to call Chasity under the circumstances that she may feel like the only reason he's calling her was because he needed something. The truth of the matter was, if there was one person that would always come to his rescue when he needed them most, it was Chasity. As much as he wanted to sit and really think on if it's worth dialing her number, procrastination had no room in his life at this very moment. His mind was racing, plus he was really worried about his sister because she was a good girl, probably never even been in a fight before. Dialing Chasity's number, to his surprise she answered on the very first ring. Made Rashad feel like she'd been waiting on his call ever since she stormed out of his Grandmother's house.

"What you want? The bitch pussy can't be hitting on none if you still using my number," Chasity said.

"Ain call to play, my mama just called and told me Aleysia just got jumped on. I need you," said Rashad.

"I'm on the way," were the only words that came from Chasity lips before the phone disconnected. Being that Rashad wanted to be prepared for any circumstances he felt as if he may need to bring Neko along as well. Rashad had no intentions of going to Clayton County and starting any altercations, but he wasn't sure what to expect. After calling Neko and explaining the situation, Neko insisted that he come. Maybe thirty minutes later, Chasity honked the horn for Lil John John and Rashad to come outside. Once the two got inside the car, Rashad told her to go to Allen Temple to get Neko. From Allen Temple, they head straight to Clayton County in Chasity mom's black 2006 Infinity 4 door sedan, driving 100 mph the entire time as if police don't exist.

Chapter 10. *No Regrets*

The black Infinity turned into Rashad's mother's neighborhood and he instantly got a weird feeling.

"Man, I hate coming out here. I can't wait till my mama move and get the hell on. The worst memories of my life came from out here and if it was up to me I'll never come back but family first," said Rashad as if he's thinking out loud. The black Infinity arrived in front of Rashad mom's home as everyone in the car noticed a group of people standing in the middle of the street two houses down, which turns into a cul-de-sac. Rashad's little sister who was 16, stood at the bottom of the their mom's driveway along with three of her girlfriends while his mom stood at the top of the driveway next to the mailbox with a sky blue sun dress on. Immediately after opening the passenger side front door all Rashad could hear was…"Yea we did it! Yea we did it! We just beat that lil bitch up and we'll do it again!" say the next-door neighbors.

Rashad couldn't believe his ears and was immediately put in a mind state of anger. They were talking about his precious little sister. What else was he left to do? He was heartbroken because his sister wasn't even that type of girl. She was the good girl, prissy type, more into her looks and books than anything. Fighting was the last thing on her mind and the disrespect was off the charts.

"Rashad don't you go over there! Come in the house! Rashad! I know you hear me!" said his mom.

After what his ears just heard concerning his little sister no one was going to be able to stop him, not his mom, or even God himself. It was more people in the crowd than the few people Rashad had with him but that was the last thing on his mind. As Rashad gets closer to the loud talking disrespectful neighbors, three of them enter their home and came back out within ten seconds. Overlooking some of the movement coming from the crowd, Rashad approached the first dude in his reach, "So you bitch made niggas like to jump on girls huh?"

FOW!!!

Out of nowhere Rashad was hit in the face by this bad body having female who was standing to the left of the person he was confronting. Chasity responded with a punch of her own that landed right in the attacker's eye. The chaos had begun and it was now a brawl from the middle of the cul-de-sac, to the hood of innocent cars, back to the neighbor's front lawn. Anybody that didn't ride in the black Infinity was an enemy and within a blink of an eye Rashad looked to his left to notice the neighbors are attempting to drag Chasity into their home by her hair while she was taking punches to the face. Rashad ran towards her as he tried to protect her and get hit with a surprise, he's stabbed directly in the center of his heart with a butcher knife! They were setting him up to come onto their property, so they could have the right to use deadly force. Rashad's adrenaline rush was pumping and since there was so much chaos surrounding his vision at the moment, he didn't realize their plan.

Suddenly, Neko ran over to smash the female dragging Chasity by her hair in the head with a plant pottery, which broke into pieces due to the force. Losing blood by the second, Rashad looked to his right and noticed Lil John John brawling with someone taller and heavier than he was holding a 4 feet steel pole but from the looks of it, Lil John John was not letting up.

Unexpectedly, everyone against Rashad and Da Crew tried to run inside the neighbor's home to take cover but the damage was already done. Rashad and Lil John John both had tunnel vision, which forced Lil John John to chase behind the attacker whom was bashing him in his forehead with the steel pole and it led him right into the attacker's home. During this moment, Rashad had yet to notice that his heart had been punctured.

Once inside the home Lil John John was going wild and wanted revenge for the blood that was gushing out of his forehead caused by a steel pole. As Rashad tried to pull Lil John John from the brawl that had spilled into the home, he was stabbed in his heart for the second time, inches from the first wound. It was apparent that they were trying to kill him. Not able to believe what his eyes are seeing, Neko was appalled as he stood in the middle of the street looking around and confused as if he were dropped off on a planet full of aliens. Rashad was losing pints of blood by the second and had yet to realize he's been stabbed in his heart twice with a butcher knife. By the time he realized it, he was face first on the concrete. Hitting the concrete with as much force as he did created a hole underneath the facial hair on his chin. Not realizing what was happening, he got back up within three seconds but fell down on his back.

At this moment, Lil John John was out of the neighbor's home, Chasity was on her feet, and Neko was fully aware of his surroundings. He even noticed the neighbors that just attacked them had cut off every single light inside the home as if no one was there, including the porch light. Somehow Rashad was moved from the street onto the neighbor's lawn directly across the street from his mother's home. Luckily, that particular neighbor had nursing experience and could at least give Rashad half the help he so desperately needed.

"Oh my God, he's losing too much blood!" screamed the neighbor.

As everyone looked at Rashad's bloody shirt in shock, Lil John John loses it, "Man fuck! I can't lose another brother to these streets, they got me fucked up!" He ran to the black Infinity to get Rashad's chrome 38 Revolver with the maple wood handle, which was under the passenger seat. As Lil John John attempted to open the car door, he realized the outside of both wrists were sliced to the bone past the white meat. He had every reason to panic or pass out, but he didn't. Instead, he kept his composure and ran inside Rashad mother's home to get a better view of the horrific site, being that it was so dark outside.

Meanwhile, as Rashad lay on the neighbor's lawn, everyone tried their best to keep his eyes open. Jake, Rashad's youngest brother ran out of the house with a huge pan of water to throw on Rashad's body, thinking it would make his condition better.

"Jake, No! If that water gets into his bloodstream he may die!" yelled the neighbor.

"Please don't die on me! I love you with everything in me," Chasity said dramatically as she tried her best to look in Rashad's eyes.

"Oh my God!" yelled his mom. Rashad's mother was put in such shellshock that she shitted herself in front of everyone, literally, but no one was aware of it besides herself. Standing with a sundress on made it no better and from the pain her eyes are witnessing, shitting on herself was the last thing on her mind, as well as wearing a dress while doing so. She really thought she was watching her oldest son die right in front of her eyes. Silence came from Neko, as he stood in similar pain as Rashad's mom. "Baby just focus on breathing. Y'all make sure he doesn't close his eyes!" yelled the neighbor as she stressed how important keeping his eyes open was to the onlookers and those words were the last Rashad heard before waking up in ICU inside of Grady Memorial Hospital located in downtown Atlanta.

Chapter 11. *Grady Hospital*

"Hi, Mr. Thomas! God has really blessed you!" Rashad woke up in the hospital bed oblivious to what was going on, not even aware of where he is. The doctor noticed he was confused by the look on his face.

"You've been in intensive care for 6 days Mr. Thomas. Do you remember what happened to you?" asked the nurse. Rashad remained quiet, not realizing his father along with his father's friend were both in the room with him. He glanced to the left of him where he noticed his dad shedding tears. Rashad had never witnessed his father cry and although Rashad didn't know the reason, he was soon to find out. Rashad tried to move but any movement felt like his skin was ripping apart.

"Whoa! Mr. Thomas, you have to take it easy! You just underwent open-heart surgery and have numerous lacerations all around your body. I need you to be careful and cautious of how you move. You've been unconscious for quite some time, so I'll step out for a minute to give you time with your family. I'll be back shortly, by the way, I'm nurse Jacky and I will be assisting you until told otherwise," said the nurse. Immediately after she walked out, Rashad opened up his hospital gown to see 32 staples going down his chest. They were placed there after surgery to keep his chest from detaching itself from each side. Rashad couldn't believe what his eyes were seeing but that was nothing compared to what he had in store.

"Son, you can't be doing me like that, you know better than that shit. You know not go to nobody else side of town with the bullshit, you make them bring it to you." Rashad watched as his father speaks with tears running down his face showing pain and sorrow. Street dude, never had a 9 to 5 and besides having a tough childhood, lived above average majority of his life, which gave him many reasons to smile. That was until he got the call that his oldest son had been viciously hurt and may not live to see another day. Majority of Rashad's entire family was downstairs in the lobby and couldn't wait to see him.

Once Rashad sat up in the bed with the help of his dad, he's able to gather some thoughts being that he remembered only a little.

"Where Neko them at?" he asked. Which happened to be the first words to come out of his mouth since waking up from ICU. "They should be at home now. Atlanta Medical took them in because they were the best fit for their injuries. You came to Grady because this is the best hospital in Atlanta for Trauma," Rashad's father explained.

"Why would they take them to Atlanta Medical? Why would they split us up?" Rashad started to panic as he began overthinking about what may have gone wrong.

"I just know everybody got hit but you caught the worst end of the stick. That's all I know," said his dad as he replied to Rashad's questions.

Knock, Knock, Knock…

Knocking before opening the door, not waiting on anyone to tell her to come in, is Chasity. As she walked into the hospital room to lay eyes on Rashad, she held her hand up to her face covering her mouth in disbelief that Rashad was still breathing.

"That bitch and her family tried to kill you and then got on the news talking about she was the only one with a knife. Bitch please!" said Chasity.

"Son, I'm going downstairs to tell everybody you up. We been here for days waiting on you to wake up. God is good!" Rashad's father said in excitement. Once he left the room along with his friend, Rashad wanted to be filled in on everything.

"So, what you talking bout? What bitch and what news? What the fuck happened?" he asked.

"Huh? You don't remember getting stabbed? Getting airlifted by the helicopter? Being in the hospital for a week before you even opened your eyes today?" Chasity said as she tries to summarize this tragic situation.

"From the looks of these thick ass water hole tubes coming out of my body I'm sure something happened, but I just can't remember what. I do remember having words with my mother's neighbor but that's all I remember," Rashad replied.

"Well, Neko got cut in the face, close to his temple. Somehow, I got cut behind my ear. Lil John John got cut on the outside of both wrists, deep enough to see white meat and his bones. You on the other hand, got hit in your heart twice with a butcher knife, once directly on the center, and once above your left ribs. The doctor been telling us that if you do make it, more than likely you'll be brain dead with great memory loss but fuck him. He can't control God's work and from the looks of it my baby doing just fine!" Rashad was far from brain dead but the part about having great memory loss was an understatement.

Knock… Knock… Knock… It's nurse Jacky and she was coming to tell Rashad that he was about to be transferred to a bigger room for his family. Rashad had a nice size family so a bigger room was very much needed and they were all anxious to see him.

"Your dad's side of the family has been giving your mom a hard time due to the situation. They blaming her for everything that happened to you so be prepared for the drama," Chasity said. Although Chasity was getting

Rashad caught up on the family drama as well as the incident that recently occurred, she couldn't prepare him for the pain and horror he had coming his way no matter how much she wanted to.

"Mr. Thomas, it may cause you a little pain but I need for you to try and get into this wheelchair so it'll be easier for you to make it through the hospital room doors," said the nurse.

Chasity and the nurse both tried to help Rashad out of the bed by helping him bend his back first so he could bring his legs around then off the bed.

"Ahhhhhh! I can't do it!" yelled Rashad. To bend his back would only cause severe pain for him which was understandable being that he hasn't moved a muscle in 6 days and the surgery performed on his body made it no better.

"Witnessing what you just went through, you can do anything! Now get yo ass up and get in this chair!" Chasity said demandingly. Of course, she couldn't feel his pain, hell, it wasn't many people in the hospital that could, but watching Rashad hurt made her hurt as well. Rashad didn't realize it quite yet but trying to at least move his muscles was better than not moving them at all. He would also become stronger if he tried to move around more as well as stretching his muscles, which are so tight and tense at the moment.

The cursing and yelling coming from Rashad wasn't close to enough to stop either nurse Jacky or Chasity from getting him out of the bed and into that wheelchair. At the same time, they had to be extremely careful with every movement involving him because he had four chest tubes hanging from the inside of his body. One tube attached to his left lung, one tube attached to his right lung, one tube attached to his left kidney, and one tube attached to his right kidney. The tubes connected to his kidney were much smaller than the tubes attached to his lungs, but they were all being held together with staples and thread. If a child didn't know any better, they would have mistaken him for "Octopus Man."

Rashad was now sliding down the hallway in his wheelchair being pushed by Nurse Jacky. He heard voices of his family members coming down the hallway as if they're the only people on the 6th floor. Approaching his new room, Rashad instantly noticed it was almost a family reunion. He also noticed his new room had space for an extra patient but that area was empty at the moment. Rashad was surprised to see as many faces in show of support and had yet to realize the pain and agony he had given his family over this past week. Excited as his family was to see him, Rashad's feelings were not mutual.

"Nephew!!! I thought we lost ya for a minute! I was gone ride this wheelchair all the way down the expressway and fuck some up bout you!" Uncle Kennyman said.

"And they talking bout my cousin was gone be brain dead! Better let em know cuz, prayers go up and blessings come down!" said Mondu, his older cousin that stays in Allen Temple.

As Rashad's family helps him out of his wheelchair and onto the bed, he tried his best to get comfortable. Ms. Tara, Rashad's mother tried to feed him a slice of bread being that he'd been eating through a tube in ICU for 6 days, which he didn't remember. Taking the slice of bread, he looked around the hospital room and looked at each family member in their eyes one by one. He then took a bite of the bread, looked at the 10-inch scar going down his chest that was being held together with staples, and lifts up the chest tube that's attached to his right lung. The thick chest tube leads to a special made box shaped machine, which monitors how much unwanted fluid was coming out of the lung, while pumping it up at the same time being that both lungs collapsed due to his stab wounds.

Rashad examined the chest tubes, got a good look of the yellowish, brownish fluid flowing through it, then reality hit. He suddenly picked his head up, looked out the window where the sun was peeking through, and abruptly burst out in tears. Rashad was mentally depressed and couldn't believe the situation he's in was real life. He was hoping it's all a dream but it wasn't and the sun shining through the hospital window made him accept the reality. Although his injuries are severe, things could be much worse— he could be dead.

Rashad's family was so excited to see him but when they finally seen him and the depressed state that he was in, it switched their mind state and mood from happiness, to anger, and hate towards the people that put their family in his situation. They never pictured him to be as sad as he was and probably never even witnessed him shed a tear at all outside of a funeral. He was at a all-time low point in his life and the depression put him to sleep right after breaking down in front of his immediate family. Rashad needed time alone and it was obvious, so when he dozed off, a few family members left while a few slept in the waiting area.

After a few hours of sleep, Rashad woke to the touch of his mother's hand on his shoulder. It was time for him to get acquainted with the head doctor in charge and there he was, short Asian dude or maybe Chinese standing 5'4" at the end of Rashad's bed where his feet were. Alongside three interns with a notepad in everyone's hand.

"Hi, Mr. Thomas I'm Dr. Kwon and I'll be the head doctor for your procedure. How are you doing?" Rashad looked at him in the eyes and said not one word. Ms. Tara, Rashad's mom looked at him with her watery, puffy eyes and said, "Son, please talk to these doctors, I know you hurt and probably very mad with me, but I need you to talk to these doctors." Rashad's actions were bothering his peers in such an impacting and depressive way and they couldn't hide it. He noticed it when his mom said, "you're probably very mad with me," when deep down he wasn't.

It just wasn't as easy for him to cope with being stabbed in the heart with a butcher knife as if it were an every other day type occasion.

"I apologize doc, it's just kind of hard adjusting to my situation you know?"

"Mr. Thomas, you've been stabbed in your heart twice with a butcher knife, lost four pints of blood, both lungs collapsed, and we've lost your heart beat twice. Not wanting to talk to me is totally understandable. These intelligent young people beside me are interns. I will be your primary doctor here at Grady Hospital and it's my job to make sure you become stronger, physically, and internally," said Dr. Kwon.

"I understand Doc, and I appreciate you for overlooking my stubborn ways. Dealing with this shit ain't easy," Rashad responded.

"I totally understand and I'm here for you whenever you need me. How are you feeling right now? Scale 1-10 what's your pain?" Dr. Kwon asked.

"I'm at a 7 right now and every time I stretch it's like I'm tearing my skin doc. I be scared to move," Rashad said.

"You have to remember that your chest has been cut open, not to mention the left and right side of your body has been cut open as well to attach chest tubes to your lungs. The surgeons either used staples or needles and thread to keep the tubes in place so it will take time adjusting to," said Dr. Kwon.

"It didn't take for you to say that for me to figure that out a long time ago. I need pain pills on standby doc."

"I'm sure you do and your nurse will surely compensate you with them. In the meantime, you take it easy Mr. Thomas and get you some rest. Try to clear your mind and reframe from all things that will raise your blood pressure or cause your heart to race because that's the last thing you need. I'm going to check on some other patients and I wish you the best on your recovery," Dr. Kwon said as he ended the conversation.

As Dr. Kwon walked out the room, leaving behind Chasity, Ms. Tara, Rashad's dad, and his Grandma Betty. This would be there first time that Rashad's mom and his dad's side of the family were in the same room since awakening from ICU and the tension was so thick you could cut it with a knife. Although tension lingered around the room, Rashad didn't want to hear one word about blaming his mother and it was written all over his face so he didn't have to say it for them to see it.

"Well I need to go home and pack some clothes. So who gone stay down here with him for the night?" Ms. Tara asked.

"I will!" Chasity said.

Grandma Betty had a look on her face as if she couldn't bear the thought of leaving Rashad alone with Chasity while in his condition, being that she'd seen the two argue, fuss, and fight more than often. Rashad wasn't expecting his father to stay the night because he was sure he had money to chase, the hustle was 24/7 and Rashad understood that. Grandma Betty wanted to stay but she had to go to work in the a.m. plus she knew that if it were left up to Rashad, he would choose Chasity anyway. The decision was made and Chasity wasn't going anywhere. Everyone that was left in the room gave Rashad their hugs and kisses then headed home. With his cell phone lying on his left side, sitting on the mobile food table given to him, Rashad began to take pictures of the scars and wounds all over his body.

Chapter 12. *Reaction Behind Every Action*

9:30 a.m. The phone vibrates before Rashad notices Lil John John was calling.

"Wake yo ass up foo! I'm bout to come eat breakfast wit ya," said Lil John John.

"Come on wit it! I been up since 6 this morning looking out this damn window, ain even cut the TV on yet," Rashad responded.

"It's all good foo, be patient you'll be home real soon. I'll be down there to fuck wit ya in minute."

Obviously the conversation between the two friends woke Chasity up because Rashad hung up the phone to realize she was up staring at him with a smirk on her face.

"You have 32 staples in your chest," Chasity said.

"How would you know?" Rashad asked.

"Because crazy, I counted them when you went to sleep last night."

"Let me find out you being weird while I sleep," Rashad said in a jokingly manner.

It'd been a week since Rashad had awaken from ICU, which made it two weeks in all and Chasity had been by his side the whole time. She even wiped his ass a few times when he couldn't and being in his situation made him appreciate that a lot. Sitting in the pastel green reclining chair to the right side of his hospital bed, Chasity turned and said, "Look bay, I need to go home and regroup. These little showers don't give me no justice in this hospital," Chasity said. She needed time to herself and she deserved it. Even though Rashad didn't want her to leave, Chasity had a life of her own outside of Rashad and that was something he had to accept. She was a senior in high school and had just been fired from Red Lobster due to the altercation that took place a few weeks ago.

"That's cool bay, you been doing your part and I'll be a fuck nigga to try and hold you hostage," said Rashad.

Chasity was the only person able to keep him sane during his visit and it took no rocket scientist to realize it.

"My mom just text me and said she's ten minutes away so I'm going downstairs and wait for her." Minutes after Chasity exits the room, a knock was heard from the outside of Rashad's hospital room door.

Walking in without an invite was Nurse Jacky, "Hey Mr. Thomas. You already know the routine, 1 blood thinner and 2 Percocet," which he could only take every four hours to prevent overdose and his moment to order breakfast. That's only if he had the appetite for it.

"I'm sick of these blood thinners Ms. Jacky. Do I have to keep taking them every morning?" Rashad asked.

"You can refuse them if you want but I wouldn't suggest it. These blood thinners or as we call them, 'lovenox' are used to treat blood clots, prevent blood vessels complications, chest pains, and heart attacks. You may not like them, but I assure you that these blood thinners are making your hospital visit much easier than it would be without them."

"Well no more complaints about blood thinners from me," Rashad said with a change of mind.

"Yea I bet," Nurse Jacky replied. The sense of humor made them both laugh. "So, no breakfast this morning?" she asked.

"Naw my appetite still dry Ms. Jacky, I'll take some apple juice though."

"Apple juice it is then," says Nurse Jacky before she left the room. Seconds later, Lil John John came in right behind her.

"There go my muthafuckin dawg!" Rashad said with much excitement; being that this was the first time seeing Lil John John since being in the hospital. They'd talked on the phone numerous occasions since Rashad had been down and out but this was the first time seeing each other face to face. The first thing Rashad noticed was both of Lil John John's arms had casts on them from the elbow down, which only allowed him to see Lil John John's fingernails on each hand with his thumbs poking out. Rashad also noticed a two-inch scar going down Lil John John's forehead being held together with stitches and staples.

"Damn bro, how you been washing yo ass?" Rashad asked.

"I haven't nigga, my mama been doing it for me. All these hoes claim they fuck wit me but none of them bitches came through and checked on me yet," Lil John John said.

"Damn bro, so how long you supposed to have the cast on?"

"Supposed to be six months, that's if I wait that long before I take this shit off myself. It's helping me but the longer I keep it on, the longer my arm remains stiff and I don't need that. My arms ain't broke, my wrists just fucked up," Lil John said as he expressed his dislike for the cast that was placed on him to support his wrists.

"Fuck all that though, we still alive. What you tell them detectives when they came down here?" Lil John John asked.

"Detectives? What detectives?" asked Rashad.

"Oh okay, I see they talked to everybody but you. Wonder what they got up they sleeve? I really feel like the justice system against us foo…"

"What make you say that?" Rashad asked with a concerned look on his face.

"Because bro that bitch got on the news telling lies, talking bout we came from Atlanta to Clayton County to fight her son, and we kicked her door in looking for him. She got them crackers looking at us like we a gang and the suspects when we really the victims," Lil John John said in no playing matter.

"That's what that bitch said?" Rashad asked looking confused.

"Hell yea! That shit came on the news! She know she fucked up so it's basically our word against hers right now but as long as we got God we gone be good. I didn't come down here to run you crazy though. How you been feeling foo?" Lil John John asked.

"Depressed, begging the nurse for Percocet every thirty minutes knowing I can only take two every four hours. Tossing and turning every night trying to get comfortable knowing I can't do shit but lay on my back. Shit driving me crazy bro! I can't even wash up how I want to because I have so many open wounds on my body. My nuts and ass clean but I'm musty as fuck due to the holes that were created for the chest tubes being so close to my armpits. This might sound crazy bro but if I had a choice to choose thirty days in jail or thirty days being where I'm at right now, tell them folks to bring them cuffs."

"Nigga you talking crazy," said Lil John John. "Yea, you in here but at least you got your freedom. I understand shit ugly, but I don't ever want to hear no bullshit like that again." The words spoken by Lil John John made Rashad man up just that fast and it was a good thing, coming from his right-hand man rather than coming from someone that Rashad wouldn't listen to.

Lil John John kicked it with Rashad for about two hours before he realized he had a doctor's appointment coming up shortly for his injuries.

"I'm bout to get up out of here foo. Got a doctor's appointment at Atlanta Medical to get these cast replaced with fresh ones. Have you been praying?" Lil John John asked.

"Don't ask me no shit like that, without him I'm nothing," Rashad replied.

"That's what I wanna hear! Keep ya head up bro, you'll be out of here in minute. Love ya foo," were the last words spoken by Lil John John before he exited Rashad's hospital room. Rashad needed that company from his friends and peers because they were the only people to give him the energy and strength to become stronger whether they knew it or not. Drinking his apple juice brought to him by Nurse Jacky, Rashad watched as a brown skin baldhead man with hospital attire walked and stood in front of his hospital bed.

"Mr. Thomas?"

"Yes, that's me," Rashad responded.

"How are you doing?"

"I could be better…" expressed Rashad.

"I'm sure. Well to start off, my name is Mr. Powell and I'm your lung specialist. I was sent here to remove the tube from your right lung. Your primary head doctor, Dr. Kwon feels as if your right lung is much healthier than your left lung but it's only one way to find out. I need to make sure you're okay with this procedure before I proceed."

"Hell yea I'm ready but where's the rest of your team? You supposed to be doing this by yourself?" Rashad asked nervously.

"Yes, this is my job and I'm great at what I do. It's not as complicated as you think. All you do is take a deep inhale until I tell you to hold your breath, that very moment I will snatch the tube out, but you will continue to hold your breath until I patch your wounds, so no extra air will get into your lungs. Once we finish, you will go to the X-ray room to make sure this procedure went as planned. If the X-ray shows any excess air in your lungs, the surgeons will be forced to insert the tube back into your lung and I don't want that for you. So, let's get it right the first time so you can avoid any future problems. Are you ready?" Mr. Powell asked.

"No, I'm not but at the end of the day it's not about what I want, it's about what I need. With that being said, I'm ready whenever you are," Rashad said.

"Well let's get started. I know you can't lay completely on your left side because of the chest tube attached, but I need you to turn over as much as you can so I can get the best view of your right lung."

Rashad was as nervous as a little boy walking home from school after the principal had just called his mom and it was all on his face. Three minutes in, Mr. Powell was cutting the stitches from Rashad's skin, which held the tubes in place when Rashad hears, "Are you ready?" He could have shitted on himself, but it was now or never and right now he had to suck it up and be a man.

"Yea doc, come on wit it!" Rashad said eager to get the horrific scene over with.

"When I get to 1, you will hold your breath until I tell you to breathe. 3...2... Inhale!" *Yank!* Mr. Powell had snatched the tube. "Continue to hold your breath!!!" yelled Mr. Powell. Although it felt like a snake crawling through Rashad's body, it wasn't half as much pain as he expected.

"You can breathe now," Mr. Powell said as it took him 30 seconds at the most to patch up the wound. Adjusting to the pain, Rashad didn't have much energy to even give Mr. Powell thanks. After all, he didn't even know if the procedure went according to plan.

Shortly after the procedure, Nurse Jacky walked in to spot Rashad sleeping like a baby. Of course she wanted him to get rest but it was important that they find out if the procedure that taken place earlier was done correctly. Tapping on his shoulder, "Mr. Thomas... Mr. Thomas, I need you to get up. I know you're tired, but we have to go get an X-ray."

Chapter 13. *God Gives His Strongest Battles To His Strongest Soldiers*

Ring... Ring... Ring... Rashad turned over as much as possible to catch his Grandma Betty's phone call before she hung up. "Hey baby! Your mom told me that they took the tube out your right lung. How you feeling? What did the X-ray show?"

"I'm still in a lot of pain but I'm feeling better. The X-ray shows that my right lung is healthy. It still has some healing to do but it's not as bad as it was two weeks ago. I'm just hoping my left lung makes the same recovery. Where Kennyman at? Ain heard from him," Rashad asked curiously.

"He in there watching TV. He say he called you but you didn't answer," Grandma Betty said.

"He probably did while I was sleep, you just woke me up with your call. I'll call him back when I get off the phone with you," Rashad said.

"So have you been reading the Bible I left?"

"No, but I've been praying," Rashad replied.

"Well that's good baby, just read it when you have the free mind to do so. I know you're going through a lot, but there is no problem that God can't solve, never forget that. I was just calling to check up on you and to congratulate you on the X-ray results. I love you and I'll see you later!" said Grandma Betty.

"I love you too!" Rashad expressed from the bottom of his heart. Soon after the conversation ended, Rashad placed a call to his uncle Kennyman.

"Nephew!!! How you doing?"

"Unk!!! I miss you man. This hospital shit got me so depressed and fucked up I just can't shake this shit! I got to have someone help me with everything I do! I can't take no showers or get in the tub because water may seep inside my body. Not to mention I got to keep a urine jug next to my bed to piss just in case I can't make it to the bathroom fast enough. Shit just starting to fuck with me mentally."

"Nephew I know how you feel. Now you see what I've been going through the last 25 years of my life. At least you can feel, nephew; I can't feel nothing below the waist, but I'm alive and healthy. You gone be okay nephew, the hard part over with. Get you some rest and take it one day at a time," said Uncle Kennyman.

"Right and I respect you so much for that unk. This situation made me realize how much of soldier and how strong you really are mentally. I don't want to ask nobody for shit! But I have to because I really need help and it's not much that I can do by myself so I can only imagine how you feel 7 days a week, 365 days a year. You too solid," Rashad said.

"Yea nephew it gets tough sometimes, but God gives his strongest battles to his strongest soldiers and don't ever forget it," Uncle Kennyman said.

"With all these scars on my body the last I'm gone do is forget that one! I love ya unk but let me get off this phone so I can call for some Percocet, this pain starting to kick in."

"Alright nephew, get ya rest. I'll be down there one day this week to kick it wit ya. Love ya boy."

Immediately after hanging up the phone, oxycodone was the only thing on Rashad's mind. The pain came unexpectedly fast at times and when it did, it hit hard. Since becoming so comfortable with Nurse Jacky, the hree-digit extension number used to reach her doesn't get an answer. The pain Rashad was experiencing right then had blinded him from the big black bold letters wrote on the marker board that reads, Nurse Penny, Overnight Nurse; Ext 457. Now that his panic level began to drop a few notches, his pain continued to rise.

Rashad had the choice to choose between morphine or Percocet but never both at once. The morphine was much stronger than Percocet but it didn't last as long. To insert morphine into Rashad's body, it would be injected into his IV tubes. The fact that injecting the morphine burns a little at the beginning of the process usually caused him to take Percocet instead. Rashad just didn't find the sense for him to go through pain in order to relieve some. Finally getting in touch with Nurse Penny, she wasted no time getting the pain relieving pills to her patient.

Being this was Rashad's first time meeting Nurse Penny since being in the hospital, he assumed that Nurse Jacky's hours were cut short to give her a little personal time to herself. He wasn't completely sure if that was the case and didn't really care as long as he had Percocet by his side. As Nurse Penny introduced herself while trying to build a connection they both hear a knock at the door, it was Chasity. Once Rashad noticed who was walking through the door, a smile appeared on his face that no one could give him, which made him forget Nurse Penny was in the room. Walking towards the hospital bed approaching Rashad, a musty odor hits Chasity nose immediately!

"Oh naw, you bout to get your ass up! Smelling like you scared of water," she said. Ten minutes later Chasity was washing Rashad's whole body head to toe, balls to the wall, even his ass. It boosted Rashad's ego knowing that his girlfriend was willing to wipe his ass and take on the role of his mom without having a problem doing it. Although that was the love he needed, mentally she was molding him to be a sucker for love in the future due to the memories from their past.

Now that Rashad has company, he's not as depressed as he would be if he were alone. Chasity gave him happiness as well as energy and he couldn't hide it, so he decided to turn on the television being that it hadn't been on since yesterday. Once he turned on the television, which it was already on the local news channel, he noticed big bold letters sliding across the bottom of the screen reading "BREAKING NEWS." A young African American teenager by the name of Trayvon Martin was fatally shot in Florida while unarmed by a neighborhood watch volunteer. The volunteer that committed the murder went by the name of George Zimmerman. Rashad and Chasity had yet to realize that they were witnessing the beginning of an epic movement, "Black Lives Matter."

Chapter 14. *Trayvon Martin*

Rashad had been stabbed in his heart twice with a butcher knife, lost four pints of blood, was in ICU for four days, and was airlifted by a helicopter because the ambulance van would not have made it to the hospital in time. Although Rashad was blessed to see another day, he could relate so much to Trayvon Martin because the people that cut him up were claiming self-defense as well but were lying. The case was a lot similar to Rashad's, which was the reason why the case had every piece of his attention.

Trayvon Benjamin Martin was born on February 5, 1995. God called him home February 26, 2012. Trayvon was an African American from Miami Gardens, Florida, who, at 17 years old, was fatally shot by George Zimmerman, a white Hispanic neighborhood watch volunteer, in Sanford, Florida. Trayvon, who was serving a school suspension, had gone with his father on a visit to his father's fiancée at her townhome. On the evening of February 26, 2012, Trayvon went to a convenience store to purchase a pack of Skittles candy and a canned Arizona drink. As Trayvon returned from the store, he walked through a neighborhood that had been victimized by robberies several times that year. George Zimmerman, a member of the community watch, spotted him and called the Sanford Police to report him for suspicious behavior. Even after being told by police to stay in his vehicle and wait until police arrived, George Zimmerman didn't listen. He continued to follow Trayvon Martin on his own terms.

Moments later, there was an altercation between the two individuals in which Zimmerman shot Trayvon in his chest. Zimmerman was not charged at the time of the shooting by Sanford Police, who said there's no evidence to deny his claim of self-defense. After national media focused on the tragedy, being that there was no evidence that shows Trayvon even had a life-threatening weapon to put Zimmerman's life in danger, George Zimmerman was eventually charged and tried in Trayvon's death. A jury acquitted Zimmerman of murder and manslaughter. He was innocent of all charges and now a free man. Rashad nor Chasity could believe their ears or eyes. Another young African American had been murdered in cold blood for being in the wrong place at the wrong time, while being black and we have yet to receive justice.

Rashad's phone rings, he looked to see it's his mother and after speaking just one word Rashad could tell that she already had a little liquor in her system.

"Rashad! Do you see this shit!? George Zimmerman is not guilty!" she said. "Yea I'm watching it now, ma. This shit getting crazy. The racism getting out of hand, but retaliation gone take its course soon," Rashad said.

"No! Fuck That! His mama needs justice! Hell, I need justice! My baby been in the hospital going on three weeks now and I'm sick of this shit! That bitch tried to take you from me and I hate her for that! I can kill her myself for what she did to you! You didn't deserve that!"

The acquittal of George Zimmerman touched the black community in many different ways. Being that Rashad was in critical condition and had to fight so hard for his life, the murder of Trayvon Martin gave his mother flashbacks. She was having a breakdown mentally and physically. One hour later, approximately 1:00 A.M. Rashad's mother was at the hospital furious and angry. As she walked into Rashad's hospital room, he could feel the emotion and tension before she even spoke a word. Chasity was in the reclining chair next to Rashad's bed while Nurse Penny was in the room accommodating to his needs.

"So what's the problem? Why is my son still in this hospital? When is he coming home? I'm sick of seeing my son like this! I'm sick of this shit! I need answers!" Mrs. Tara said. She was losing it, but who could blame her?

She then takes a look at Chasity and said, "You need to go home, it is getting late. You need to call you a ride and if you can't find one I'll take you myself."

"Ma how you just gone walk in here and make decisions that best fit you? I'm grown, and she's grown! She's okay where she at!" Rashad said.

"No! Chasity you need to go home! You know what, grab your things, I'll take you myself," Ms. Tara said.

Not wanting to get in between the feud, Chasity got up and did as she was told. In return, Rashad became furious at his mom for coming into the hospital being demanding as she was. Though Rashad needed all the love he could receive, the love from his family or friends could hardly compete with the girl that's sucking and fucking him while being trapped in a hospital. The truth of the matter is, Chasity wiped his ass faithfully when he couldn't, so how could you fault him? What would make his mom think taking that away from him would make him feel any better? Forty-five minutes must have passed before Rashad's mom walked through hospital room door from dropping Chasity off and he had a mouthful ready for her to hear.

"Ma that shit is not cool! I'm the one laid up in this hospital bed, not you! You always think everything is about you but it's not! I'll really appreciate it if you just stop drinking or stop coming around me with alcohol in your system! Stop drinking Ma!!!!!!"

The response to Rashad's outburst was nothing. Nothing as in pure silence, other than the noises coming from the hospital machines scattered around the room. The vibes begin to make Rashad feel bad after a while because he felt like he had hurt his mother's feelings. Regardless, deep down inside his intentions were good and the last thing he was trying to do was hurt the lady that gave him birth. She was lying in the pastel green recycling chair, balled up like a little baby with a thick sky blue threaded blanket covering her entire body head to toe. The exact space that Chasity was taking up, which was the only place in the room for someone else to sleep. After a while it became clear that his mom just wanted to spend time with him alone and no justice for Trayvon Martin reignited the fire.

The sun was rising and Rashad had spent the majority of his night looking out his hospital room window big enough to drive a car through. He spent most of his nights watching the stars in the sky and beautiful lights on certain buildings that only appear when the sun goes down. The television was cool but life outside of Grady Hospital was much better. Watching the bright stars glow up in the sky was entertaining for him and he cherished the moment. Although he was in critical condition, God still allowed him to see, being that Rashad had come in contact with a few blind individuals forced him to understand no matter the circumstances, things could always be worse.

As Ms. Tara woke up from her sleep, it was unclear whether the energy from last night was carried over into the morning. Nurse Jacky, Rashad's daytime nurse knocked on the door before walking towards his hospital bed to ask what he wanted for breakfast, which was the everyday routine for him but he wasn't hungry.

"Yes, he is. Bring him some eggs, bacon, and grits. Add some fruit or a yogurt, please." Ms. Tara said. Nurse Jacky chuckled before looking at Rashad. She then glanced back at his mom while taking the order before exiting the room. By the look on Nurse Jacky's face, she was on Ms. Tara's side and Rashad refused to go back and forth with his mom on the next day following their fallout. Exiting the restroom inside Rashad's room for her morning touchups, she mentioned to Rashad that she would be leaving soon.

"Okay now son, I'm about to go home to freshen up and change clothes. I'll call you later. I also want you to know that I don't give two fucks about what you were talking about last night. You still my son! And I will always want the best for you. I know you not a child anymore but you still my baby and don't you ever forget it. When that nurse comes back, if you don't eat anything on that plate, you better eat that damn yogurt! Now I'm through talking. I'm going to give you the space you been asking for and I'll see you later. Eat that damn yogurt!" were the last words Rashad could remember hearing before watching his mom exit the hospital room. Shortly after Ms. Tara leaves, Chasity arrived back at the hospital with no invitation as if she had a secret camera in the room waiting for Ms. Tara to leave and it made Rashad feel secure knowing that she showed up without being told to.

Walking up to Rashad without saying a word, she kissed him on his lips, and then rubbed on his balls gently before she began to give him a morning blowjob. It was better than any order he could have placed from the hospital breakfast menu. Not wanting him to nut from the blowjob, she stopped, getting on top of him to ride his dick the best way she could without causing more pain than he's already experiencing. He was in no condition for sex let the doctors tell it, but rules were always meant to be broken.

"Oh my…"

It was Nurse Jacky bringing Rashad his breakfast and from the expression on her face she hadn't witnessed as much action in years. She stopped, stared for 5 seconds at the most, put Rashad's breakfast on his portable eating tray, and then exited the room just as fast as she walked in. Chasity didn't notice because she was facing Rashad, but he caught it all. It was actually the first time Rashad put his kids inside of her and he thanked God everyday that she didn't get pregnant. After wiping off the sex with a warm rag, Chasity sat in the infamous recycling chair next to his bed. Unexpectedly, Dr. Kwon, Rashad's head doctor walked in followed by 2 interns.

"Mr. Thomas! Looking great! How are you feeling?" Dr. Kwon said as he tried to cheer Rashad up.

"I could be better but as long as I'm breathing no complaint's, I'm just ready to go home," Rashad replied.

"I assure you that I understand and today may be your lucky day. From the X-rays and heart machines, it shows that your body strength and health are improving significantly. With that being said, my team and I have agreed to pull the left chest tube from your left lung to see how it will react afterwards. How do you feel about that?" Dr. Kwon asked.

"That's great news! Let's get this shit over with doc. I'm ready!" Rashad said excitedly.

"That's good to hear. I just wanted to pass on the good news because I'm aware that you've suffered enough. Good luck on the procedure and we will be in contact soon after," Dr. Kwon responded. The morning sex that Chasity gave him couldn't come close to the feeling that was going through his body from the conversation that just transpired through him and Dr.Kwon.

"Bay you just heard that shit?" Rashad asked as he looked towards Chasity.

"You know I did. I'm so happy for you baby! Now your skinny ass can gain some of that weight back," Chasity said.

"Yea whatever, skinny niggas slang the best pipe. Your pussy said so this morning," Rashad said.

"Look at you…Folks find out they bout to get out the hospital and just don't know how to act!" Chasity said.

Chasity's comment made the both of them laugh and you could feel the happiness in the air. While Rashad was eating his breakfast, he heard a knock on the door. It was a detective working on the case and little did Rashad realize the case was much deeper than he thought.

"Hey Mr. Thomas how are you? I'm detective Tidwell, and I'm here to talk to you about your incident. Do you have some time to talk?"

Looking confused, Rashad replied, "Yea, I got time what you need to know?"

"I'm just going to ask you a couple of questions and you can answer with the best of your ability," said Detective Tidwell.

"Okay," Rashad said.

"Why were you in the neighborhood?" the detective asked.

"My mother stays out there," Rashad replied.

"Were you just stopping by to see your mother or were you called by your mother to come down to her home?"

"The fuck type question is that? A female and her brother jumped on my little sister. I was checking to see if my little sister was okay," Rashad said.

"Your blood was on your mother's neighbor's porch, which is a sign of trespassing. Any idea how your blood got on her porch?" asked the detective.

"Man, who side you on? I'm in the hospital stabbed the fuck up and you talking to me like I'm the suspect! I was stabbed twice in my fucking heart with a butcher knife! I'm sure blood was dripping from the knife everywhere! The only moment I was on that lady porch was to stop her family from dragging my girlfriend into their house!"

"How many people were in the car with you when you arrived to your mother's home?" the detective asked.

"Aye bro, I don't have no more answers for you. I can't remember shit else, get the fuck out my room," Rashad said as he began to become frustrated.

"That's fine. Good luck on your recovery," said the detective before leaving the room. The detective was clearly trying to get under Rashad's skin but from the information that he received this morning from Dr. Kwon, the bullshit that was coming out of the detective's mouth was a small thing to a giant.

Chapter 15. *Blood Is Thicker Than Water*

"Bay wake up, the lung specialist is here to remove the tube from your left lung. Let's get this shit over with," Chasity said. Taking a thirty-minute catnap, Rashad was awoken from his sleep by Chasity. Immediately after opening his eyes, Rashad noticed that it wasn't Mr. Powell, the lung specialist whom did such a great job pulling the chest tube from his right lung.

"Where is Mr. Powell?" Rashad asked.

"I'm not sure but I was called upon to do the job and I can assure you that you can trust me."

After the nurse finished talking, Rashad realized that her nametag spelled "Intern." He's instantly hesitant and asked the nurse why would they choose an intern for such an important procedure rather than an official lung specialist. The intern, a young Black American woman, could tell that Rashad was irritated by the questions he's asking and yet scared at the same time.

"Mr. Thomas I understand you're scared and nervous but I need you to calm down. I was appointed to take care of you because the people way above my position understand that I'm equipped to do the job and I need you to understand that as well."

Rashad eventually puts his guard down, while Chasity sat speechless next to him in the infamous reclining chair. His mind was telling him to call for an official lung specialist with experience but he was in such a rush to get back on his feet that he finally believed in the intern standing at the end of his bed.

"Now that I have your full attention, the procedure that's about to take place is no different from the procedure of your right lung. I will lay pads down for you to turn on the right side of your body, so your left lung is facing towards the ceiling. Do you understand the steps to this procedure, Mr. Thomas?"

"Yes, I do." Rashad replied.

"You can stay in here or you can step in the hallway," the intern said as she turned towards Chasity to explain what's about to take place.

"It's up to him," Chasity replied.

"She can stay," said Rashad.

"Okay great. Now, Mr. Thomas if you can, could you gently turn over on the right side of your body as much as possible so that the left chest tube is facing towards the ceiling," the intern said.

"Oh my God baby you're so strong! You're a soldier and don't let nobody else tell you different," Chasity said.

Those were the first words that came to mind as she watched the intern grab her utensils to prepare for the procedure. As the intern cut through the thread, which was sewed through his skin that was placed to secure the chest tubes, the only thing on Rashad's mind was that he was going home. The intern was on her final piece of thread and the moment Rashad was waiting for was finally here.

"Mr. Thomas it's now time for me to pull the chest tube out of your lung. Are you ready?"

"Yes!" Rashad said anxiously.

"Ok, I'll count to three and in between those three seconds you will take a deep breath. On three, you will continue to hold your breath until the complete tube is pulled out of your body and completely patched up. Do you understand?"

"Yes," Rashad said.

1… 2… "Wait!" said Rashad.

"What's the problem?" Ask the intern. "I'm sorry mam but I'm nervous and scared. Promise me you know what you're doing," Rashad said nervously.

"I promise, but you can't snatch away from me like that unexpectedly. You could cause more damage upon yourself than I ever could, so if we're going to go through with the procedure I will need for you to trust me and relax."

With a sigh of relief, Rashad took a deep breath in and replied with a simple, "okay."

"1… 2… inhale!" *Yank!* Rashad wants to scream but he understands the only way for him to do so is to breathe. The only option he has is to bite down and grind his teeth as hard as he could until the wound was completely patched up and the pressure he was feeling released.

"I'm so proud of you!" Chasity said.

"You can breathe now," the intern said. After just taking his first breath, Rashad noticed that something isn't right. Each breath he took caused him to hear air seeping through the patches as if he had a k-9 dog nose attached to the left side of body.

"Something not right bay. It's no reason I should be hearing air seeping out of my body like it's a tire going flat. It don't take a rocket scientist to know this shit not right," said Rashad as he expressed his dislike for the procedure to Chasity but loud enough for the intern to hear clearly.

"Mr. Thomas, I assure you that everything is fine. Dr. Kwon will be up here shortly to take you to the radiation room for X-rays," the intern said before exiting the room.

Rashad was noticeably irritated and had no words for the intern because deep down he felt as if the procedure wasn't done right. Shortly after the procedure, Rashad was taken to the radiation room to get results. The X-ray results didn't come back immediately so Rashad was forced to wait a few hours for the information. In the meantime, he had nothing to do but flip through TV channels when he's not flirting with Chasity. Although Rashad was thinking the worst, he was prepared for the best and didn't want to hear anything other than "Mr. Thomas, you're cleared to go home."

Faster than expected, Dr. Kwon, alongside 2 interns including the intern which Rashad was questionable about walked into Rashad's room.

"Tell me some good news doc…"

Rashad realizes the intern that did his procedure earlier had her head down and was not focused on the conversation, as she should be.

"Well Mr. Thomas I have good news and I have bad news…" said Dr. Kwon.

"Give me the bad news first," Rashad said.

"The bad news is the X-ray shows you still have air in your lungs, so we will have to place a chest tube back into it. The good news is…" Before Dr. Kwon could even get his words out, Rashad lost hope, instantly shoving his head between his knees while shedding heavy tears uncontrollably.

"I fucking asked her did she know what she was doing and she said yes! I fucking asked her! Why would y'all even send a fucking intern for such a serious procedure as if I'm motherfucking test dummy or some shit! I fucking asked her!" Rashad said as he goes ballistic.

"I understand that you're upset but the good news is you don't have as much air in your lungs as you started with," Dr. Kwon said.

"If your fucking intern knew what she was doing there wouldn't be any air in my lungs at all!" Rashad responded.

"Believe me, Mr. Thomas I understand your pain and not many…"

Cutting Dr. Kwon off mid-convo, "You don't feel my pain! You've never been stabbed in your heart twice with a butcher knife! Have you been in ICU for 5 days?! Have you been in the hospital with both lungs collapsed while doctors cut on you like a dead fucking animal while you alive watching them do it? You ain't never! So don't say you feel my pain because you don't!"

"You're right and I'm deeply apologetic about your struggle. Not many people suffer from the wounds that you have to live and tell about it. With that being said the more time we waste, the worst your lungs will get and it will eventually destroy your body internally. These papers I have in my hand gives us approval to re-insert the chest tube into your lung. The only difference is that you will not be asleep this time, you will be fully aware of what's going on but we can't start until you sign this paper," said Dr. Kwon.

"I'm not signing shit! Patch me up and send me home!" Rashad said angrily.

"Rashad!" screamed Chasity, "I know you mad, hell I'm mad too but you cannot go home like this. You'll be back in the hospital in a week."

"I'm not signing shit! I'm ready to go home!"

It was obvious Rashad was breaking down and Chasity realized not even her words held any weight at the moment. The only option left was to call his mom and like always she was there faster than 911 in a white neighborhood. Rashad youngest brother, Jake and little sister Aleysia was alongside with her. The three of them appeared, coming through the hospital room door breathing hard as if they were running full speed to Rashad's hospital room.

"He won't sign the papers, Ms. Tara…" Chasity said.

Looking at her son with fire in her eyes, "So what's the problem, son? You want to live, or you want to die?"

"I'm not signing no more papers, Ma," Rashad said.

"Son, please don't do me like this," his mother said as she began to shed tears and although she was pouring her heart out to her son, it just wasn't enough to get him to sign the paper. Rashad was fed up with the pain and it was all over his face.

Sitting in the hospital as long as he'd had was driving him crazy and he couldn't hide it if he wanted to. Glancing at his little sister, he realized she was crying heavier than anyone in the room and once making eye contact with her, it clicked that giving up on himself would result in giving up on his family and he loved his family more than he could ever explain. Rashad snapped back to reality, wiped the tears from his face and asked Dr. Kwon for the papers that he needed to sign. It was that moment in which he understood that nothing was more important than family and he would always need them just as much as they needed him.

Chapter 16. *Life Or Death*

Moments after the documents were signed, Rashad had yet to realize the pain he's about to experience. The chest tubes that were stuffed into his body were as thick and wide as the average water hose. The tube was also clear to monitor the blood and yellowish fluid coming out of the damaged lung. The more blood, air, and fluid sucked out, the stronger his body became. It's a process but that's the easy part. The hard part made you feel like you're in hell itself, but it had to be done. Rashad was seconds away from feeling the worst pain of his life, but this hospital visit had sucked so many tears from his eyes that he didn't have any more left to give.

"Now, Mr. Thomas we're going to numb the left side of your body where the upper rib cage is located, closest to your lung. It will not take away all of your pain, but I assure you that it takes away half of it," Dr. Kwon says.

"We'll step out son, I can't stand here watching you go through this," Ms. Tara says. As she exits the room, followed by his siblings and Chasity, all of Rashad's attention was focused on Dr. Kwon as he held a small pair of stainless steel sharp scissors. Hoping the scissors were about to be used to cut some type of paper, Rashad was wrong and about to experience a rude awakening. The scissors were used to cut a hole through his skin not far from the tube that was recently snatched out of him. Although the numbing shots were in place, on a scale 1-10 the pain was at a 9. Once Rashad lay on his right shoulder with his left lung facing the ceiling, scissors cut through his skin like construction paper and there was no turning back.

With a warning, 5 inches of the tube is stuffed into his body, slithering around like a snake until the right location was found to latch onto his lung. You could've mistaken the view for a movie scene, but it was real life. The strongest man alive would ask to be put asleep during the procedure and of course Rashad wanted that option but couldn't have it being that the procedure had to be done immediately. After tugging back and forth with the tube, the doctor in charge of finding the location of the lung whispered, "Got it" to Dr. Kwon. It was apparent he's found the location he was searching for.

The moment the tube was attached to the lung, the stitches were sewn into place like a needle stitching through clothing, which made the chest tube stable and secured. Once the tube was secured, Dr. Kwon activated the machine used to pump the lung while removing unwanted fluid at the same time. By doing so it shifted Rashad's spine, made him feel like someone was trying to suck his entire spine through the little hole maybe a thumb could fit through. The feeling lasted for five minutes at the most, then it disappeared or maybe Rashad just found a way to adapt. Going through pain was an understatement but at this point, what didn't kill him could only make him stronger. Now that the procedure was over and Rashad was patched up, all he wanted to know was how long the tube would be inserted. The thought of going home moved further away and it's draining him mentally.

"The tube will remain attached to your lung for three days. No need to keep it in as long as we did for the previous procedure because you don't have as much air or fluid inside. The process is coming along great and I'm deeply sorry for you and your troubles," Dr. Kwon said. Ending the conversation, the doctor exited the room while Rashad's family entered.

There wasn't much to talk about because it was an obviously sensitive situation. Rashad wanted rest and he needed it as much as a newborn baby.

It was nearly midnight, the room lights were off but the TV was on. Rashad had slept the whole day away due to the painful procedure his body had gone through earlier. Perfect timing, Nurse Penny walked in to give Rashad his blood thinners and Percocet. Once she exited the room, Rashad turned to his phone where he had numerous text messages and missed calls. One from his mom reading, "We left you alone to get rest. You went to sleep on us soon as the doctors left the room! We love you. Be strong and call us when you get up."

Of course he had missed calls from Chasity and a few others but the name that stood out the most was 'Lil Kirk'. Lil Kirk and Rashad became friends in high school. They met in tenth grade while gambling and shooting dice in the restroom of Benjamin E. Mays High School and been friends ever since. Lil Kirk had a wonderful spirit, had his way with the girls, and was also a great baseball player. He's book smart as well as street smart, which Rashad liked to think attracted the two, being that they both had that in common. Rashad hadn't heard from Lil Kirk in almost a year but whether Kirk knew it or not, Rashad really appreciated the fact that he was thinking about him while being in his condition. Made Rashad reminisce about all the good dice games the two had in the past. Returning his call, Lil Kirk answered on the first ring…

"My boy!" screamed Lil Kirk.

"What's up bro!?" Rashad replied.

"Man take yo ass to school! Ain't nothing in these streets but pain and losses. Go to school bro, we ain't missing shit out here. I heard what happen and couldn't believe that shit! I was just telling my folks all you want is some money… I'm glad you pulled through my boy. I just wanted to check up on ya."

"That's love bro. I'm not all the way there quite yet, but I'm getting there. Just taking it one day at a time," Rashad said.

"Be patient my boy. God kept you for a reason! Now you got to figure out what it is. In the meantime, think about going to college nigga. That shit gone keep you out the way bro I'm telling ya," Lil Kirk said.

"I got you bro, I promise I got ya," Rashad said before the ending the conversation. The conversation had given Rashad the spark he needed. Physically his body was restless and weak but mentally he was rejuvenated thanks to Lil Kirk. The three-day wait went by so fast because Rashad had the date locked in his head like a kid does Christmas on Dec 23rd. That third day was the only thing on his mind since being told how long the chest tube would remain inside of him.

Of course, Rashad's immediate family were aware of the procedure that'd taken place and it's his Grandma Betty who chose to ride the emotional roller coaster this particular day. Sitting beside Rashad in the infamous reclining chair, she read her Bible as he ate his 10-piece wing, mild with lemon pepper sprinkles combo from American Deli. The first time eating wings since this hospital visit and little did Grandma Betty know, that was Rashad's way of celebrating his departure. His spirits were at an all-time high and out of all the obstacles he had to cross during his visit, he was more than positive that this following procedure will be efficient. Especially with the doctors knowing the pain he's endured not even a whole week ago.

"Hey Mr. Thomas! I hate that we only see each other on such notice but today should be the end of this nightmare. Obviously, you know what his procedure consists of. Once my specialist is done, we will go to the X-ray room for final results and hopefully we will be sending you home tomorrow," said Dr. Kwon.

"Sounds great!" Rashad replied.

Snatching the chest tube from his lung was painful to say the least but it was nothing Rashad hasn't already experienced so it's safe to say that he wasn't caught off guard. Grandma Betty was a witness for the first time and never wanted to witness her grandson going through such pain ever again. No one knew if the procedure went according to plan, but Rashad did notice that he was patched up the right way this time. He didn't hear or feel any air seeping through the patch, which was a positive sign and gave him more hope. Once the X-ray pictures were taken, Rashad was escorted back to his room where Dr. Kwon and two different interns are awaiting. Not saying a word, looking into Grandma Betty's face gave him the answer to the results. She was shedding heavy tears while shaking her head at the same time while making eye contact with her grandson.

The chest tube had to be placed back inside of him and surprisingly he was ready. Grady Hospital was turning him into a beast, slowly and mentally to the point that pain was a piece of key lime cake to him. Going through these different experiences during his hospital visit made Rashad view life differently. The experiences made him realize that even when you're hoping for the best, at all times you should still be prepared for the worst. He began to learn life from personal experiences and for him, personal experiences were the best teacher. Rashad was told the tube would be inside of him for the following two days but he requested four, simply to be sure that his lung was officially healthy this time. Rashad's left lung has suffered three procedures while the right lung suffered one and instead of being scared, he was more confused than anything.

Tired of seeing her grandson hurt and go through such struggle, it forced Grandma Betty to leave and Rashad was okay with that because it was one of those days where he wanted space and privacy anyway. He eventually got up and walked around Grady Hospital a few times a day, while carrying the chest tube drainage machine. Besides walking around the hospital like an 80 year old with a bad back, the only option left to waste time included sleeping, looking out the window at traffic, or flipping through television channels all day.

The fourth day to go through with the procedure had arrived and Rashad wasn't as excited as he usually was for obvious reasons. Once the tube was snatched out and X-ray pictures were taken, the results were in.

"Your left lung is healthy and clear of all air and fluids!" said Dr. Kwon.

Rashad was ecstatic and couldn't thank God enough. After receiving the news, he passed it on to his immediate family and of course they were there in a hurry just to capture the smile they all pictured coming through the phone call.

Grady Memorial Hospital was home to Rashad for thirty whole days and it made him cherish the small things in life. The small things would be considered as being able to see, hear, smell, feel, but most of all, being able to walk on his own two feet with no complications. The visit made him cherish life as a whole and also helped him realize that no matter what life may throw at you, it could always be worse. Rashad was set to be released the next day, which would make it his 31st day inside of Grady Hospital. His family left him alone that night because they knew he would be home tomorrow. Hearing a knock on the door, it was Lil John John surprising Rashad with a visit after hearing the great news. Not being able to drive, he was dropped off by Grandma Betty after deciding to spend the final night in the hospital with Rashad.

After asking Rashad about his procedure and health, Lil John John couldn't help but to reminisce on this past month. "This got to be the worst year of our life. I was grinding, ran up almost $2,000. Got cut up and lost it all. Not to mention, mom's wiping my ass and bathing me. Ain't none of these hoes been here for me like they said. Then you all fucked up looking like the demolition man…" Both Rashad and Lil John John burst out laughing from the joke although it was a serious matter. It was a serious conversation, but it was time for laughter. After all, the hard part was over with.

"Naw for real though, the world gone hear bout this 'DC' shit one way or another. I don't know how long it's gone take but they gone hear bout this shit," Lil John John said with a purpose.

Chapter 17. *Home Sweet Home*

It was 6:00 a.m. as Rashad lay in his hospital bed excited to get his day started. The feeling reminded him of being a child back in middle school, anxious to show off his new clothes for the first time. The only difference being he wasn't trying to show off anything, he's just as anxious to step outside onto the concrete for the first time in 31 days. As Lil John John lay beside him in the infamous recycling chair asleep, Rashad couldn't get his mind off the time for him to be released, but he knew it would be sometime today and for him that was enough. It was also the first night he'd actually received decent sleep, being that all chest tubes were officially removed from his body. With time passing by, Lil John John awoke from his sleep attached with a growling, hungry stomach and the first thing on his mind was a Sausage Mcgriddle from the McDonald's breakfast menu.

"I'm hungry as fuck fool. You want some from McDonald's?" Lil John John asked.

"Naw, I'm good bro. I'm just ready to take my ass home."

From what Rashad was told, his dad was coming to pick the two of them up from Grady Hospital after being released. The day he'd been waiting for was finally there and he couldn't thank God enough. Arriving to give Rashad his discharge papers, Dr. Kwon presented him with a list of things to stay away from.

The list included: No drugs off the streets without an official prescription, no more marijuana or tobacco for the rest of your life, staying away from things that give you an adrenaline rush, and the most important one of them all was to try to remain stress free because being stressed out could cause the heart to stop functioning.

The list made Rashad feel like an old man trapped inside a young man's body. He wasn't even 21 yet and felt like all the fun was sucked out of him before his life even started. His heart is sewed up with thread, had numerous holes in both lungs that would heal overtime, and couldn't even take four footsteps without pausing for a break. Going through such struggle before the age of 21 will either make you or break you and it was apparent that Rashad was built to make it through even the darkest battles. Before ending the conversation between the two, Rashad offered his genuine appreciation to Dr. Kwon. Although he was put through many procedures that he felt could have been avoided, he was still alive and once being stabbed in his heart twice with a butcher knife, he refused to take that for granted.

"My intern will assist you downstairs to collect your prescription medicine that you will be sent home with and you will then be good to go! Take care of yourself Mr. Thomas." Lil John John hadn't arrived back from McDonald's so Rashad shot him a text to meet him downstairs. From downstairs they were both picked up by Rashad's dad and chauffeured back to the Westside of Atlanta! Riding down Martin Luther King, Rashad never thought he would be as excited to see some of the things that he's been surrounded around his entire life, like kids playing at the playground, or even watching a bird shit on the windshield while parked at a red light. Those little type moments brought him back in touch with life and he loved it.

Arriving to his Grandma Betty's home, Rashad couldn't wait to go lay on his queen size bed but before doing so, he was determined to wash up because the mustiness still lingered around him. Grandma Betty insisted on helping him, but he didn't feel comfortable with his grandmother washing his balls as well as his ass, so he tried the best he could to do it himself. Once finished, he headed to his room where he spots none other than Chasity laying on his bed. Apparently, she caught the news that Rashad was discharged from Grady Hospital but he wasn't the one to tell her right away because he wanted time to himself. As she lay on the bed with a blunt in her hand, she tried to pass it to Rashad.

"I can't smoke. I was told to stay away from weed for a minute," Rashad said.

"Come on bay, it's just weed. Weed can't kill you," Chaisty replied.

Pressuring Rashad to go against everything Dr. Kwon had told him to stay away from was killing his vibe. Rashad's road to recovery was serious to him and although he couldn't expect for everyone else to feel the same, he could only hope to surround himself around the ones that wanted it just as much as he did.

Chapter 18. *The Older You Get, The More The Unbelievable Things Become Believable*

It'd been four days since being released from the hospital and Rashad was sitting on the front porch enjoying the morning weather. In the midst of enjoying the fresh air, he received a call from Chasity but didn't answer. She called back to back and after ignoring the two calls, Rashad finally picks up, "Hello?"

"Rashad! The police has my house surrounded!" shouted Chasity.

"Surrounded? What the fuck have you done?" Rashad asked.

"Why you always think I've done something? I haven't did shit and they beating on my door! I'm scared!"

Immediately after expressing her fear, the phone hangs up. *Ring...Ring...Ring...* She calls back right away and after answering on the first ring, "They're coming to get y'all too!" said Chasity.

"Hang up the phone!" yelled the officer.

"I need to go put on my...!" The phone cuts off in the middle of the conversation between Chasity and the officer as if they were tussling for Chasity's phone, which put Rashad in panic mode instantly. The next thought to cross his mind was to call his mom but she was just as clueless to why the actions are taking place. The only option he felt he had was to call his dad and warn him to be prepared to help with any legal actions in case he's put in handcuffs. Minutes after hanging up the phone, police officers were at his grandmother's home banging on the burglar bar door.

As Rashad opened the door, the first thing to come out the officer's mouth was "We have an arrest warrant for Rashad Thomas." Rashad wasn't scared or nervous but rather confused and accepting the reality rather than running from it, forcing him to let the officers in. How could he suffer being stabbed in the heart twice with a butcher knife, two collapsed lungs, open-heart surgery, and thirty days inside the hospital, just to get out and be arrested four days later? His mind was racing, and he needed answers. "I just need to put on some socks," Rashad said as he spoke to the officers.

"Be careful with my motherfucking nephew! He just got out the hospital!" screamed Kennyman.

"We're going to take good care of him!" the officer said with a smile. Not being able to tell if the officers were being genuine or sarcastic, Rashad could care less. He was more interested in the charges, and the walk from the front porch to the patty wagon was enough time to hear it all. "So what are my charges sir? If you don't mind me asking."

"You're being charged with criminal trespassing, cruelty to children, felony assault and battery, as well as being looked at as a gang," the officer replied.

"A gang!? Cruelty to children? Man, what the fuck going on?"

"That's all I can tell you. I don't know the exact details, I'm just doing my job," the officer said. Walking towards the rear end of the patty wagon police van, Rashad spotted Chasity peeking through the small holes placed into the metal cage that's layered inside of the van. Entering the van, Rashad suffered slight pain as he walked up the steps on the rear end and would have to figure out how to deal with his pain without taking the Percocet that were prescribed to him while being incarcerated. Inside the van was a long metal sheet in the middle of the driver and passenger seat to separate the women from the men. They could hear each other's voices, but they couldn't see their faces.

"Are you, okay?" Rashad asked Chasity.

"Yes, but I just can't believe this shit! Have you talked to Neko or Lil John John?" Chasity asked.

"No, why?" Rashad asked.

"They're going to go get them too. I heard they bitch ass talking about it before they came to get you," Chasity said.

Not saying much in return, Rashad leaned his head on the inside of the van as he tried to get as comfortable as possible until he's able to stand. The devil was working and trying to get the best of Rashad. With all this drama happening at once so quickly, he couldn't help but to feel like everything that's transpiring was his fault and he hated the feeling. Arriving to Clayton County jail, Rashad couldn't believe he was about to be booked under his conditions. He could barely walk, had at least 4 raw wounds on his upper body that pushed blood out every few hours, and the 32 staples placed to keep his chest from ripping apart were exactly where the doctor left them. Of course, Rashad was in a lot of pain but this was the last place he wanted to show it.

Chasity was processed into the database first, followed by Rashad. Not long after taking his seat next to other people who were picked up on separate charges did Rashad hear Lil John John's voice coming through the same door he had to come through once entering the building, with a smile on his face that no one could take away. Neko was the last out of the three to make it after being picked up from his job. After sitting down to get to the bottom of what's going on, Rashad was quite relieved to find out his friends were holding him down instead of kicking him under the bus. Then again, the group of friends hadn't been incarcerated for an hour yet.

The air conditioner inside the county jail was close to blowing snow, which made Rashad regret not putting on a long sleeve shirt or tank top. As he sat with both arms inside his shirt while shivering like a baby, Chasity's name was called to switch out her street clothes for a bright orange jumpsuit, along with every other female that's been processed in the database within the last few hours. Escorted by three guards, the inmates were taken into a room that could have been seen inside by no one. Shortly after, the females exited the room looking like a group of tangerines. Catching eye contact with Rashad, he caught a vibe that his girlfriend wasn't in the same spirits as she was a few minutes ago. It was the moment reality slapped her in the face and made her realize that she's now an official inmate.

"Aww shit… She on yo ass now," Lil John John said sarcastically as he caught the look that she gave Rashad. It was no secret that Lil John John wasn't too much a fan of Chasity for numerous reasons, so to see her sad was only funny to him.

"Damn I hope I still got my job… Them folks came and put handcuffs on me right in front of my supervisor," Neko said as he shook his head making it obvious that was the only thing on his mind at the moment. The longer everyone sat in jail, the heavier everyone's problems became for Rashad shoulders, since feeling as if he's the reason everyone was going through their hardships in the first place.

"Rashad Thomas! Dominique Shell! John Whitfield! Stand up and get ready to dress out!" the officer yelled.

Once the group of friends stand up, Rashad kept his eyes glued on Chasity as she gave him this disgusted look in return. For Rashad to get to the only room used to dress out, he would have to walk directly past Chasity. After getting close enough to hear her whisper, "I don't care what you do but you better get me out of here, now." Her fears were only adding fuel to the fire, but how could he help her if couldn't even help himself? Everyone was complaining to him about their problems while blood was seeping through his gauze beneath his shirt, which he hadn't even spoke on since entering the jail. Rashad wanted his problems to be the least of everyone's worries whether he was going through chest pains, heart troubles, or whatever pain presented itself. Once changing into the orange jumpsuit, the group of men exited the backroom to notice each female was gone.

Apparently, they were taken to the women's side of the Clayton County facility, the specific area where the females serve their remaining time. Also where everything she needs to survive is located, such as bed, toilet, tissue, toothpaste, and etc. Walking through the half-mile tunnel underneath the jail, which leads to the men's facility was Da Crew and although the friends were built for whatever, this was the last place they wanted to be. Lil John John remained with 2 casts wrapped from his fingertips to his elbows. Neko had yet to heal from the cuts on his face, close to his temple, while Rashad could barely balance himself to stand straight up. It's a complete challenge for the three, but Rashad was always taught that God gives his strongest battles to his strongest soldiers.

It was day 2 inside of Clayton County's jailhouse facility and Rashad needed his Percocet more than ever. He'd had his gauze changed thanks to the jailhouse nurse, but the pain pills given to him were the weakest. Rashad hadn't placed one call to anyone because he was sure that his family was already working to bond him out. Neko was divided from his two friends as he was placed into a dorm full of unfamiliar faces. Rashad and Lil John John stuck together as they were placed inside the same dorm full of other unfamiliar inmates as well. Unacquainted with the time or knowing whether it's day or night, the only thing on Rashad's mind was Percocet and when he least expected it, the guard yelled…

"Rashad Thomas! Pack it up! You're going home!"

Two days in jail under his conditions were more than enough and he made sure to give God the praise he deserved. Before exiting the dorm, Rashad came in contact with Lil John John and all he asked was for Rashad to keep money on his phone for them to stay in contact until they were released. As he exited his dorm while walking past each and every other dorm in the men's facility, he searched for Neko whom he didn't see but he knew he would hear from him shortly.

Walking through the last door that led to the free world was Rashad with his mom parked at the end of the side-walk with a million things on her mind.

"What's going on Ma? Have you heard anything?" Rashad asked.

"Other than the charges, no, but I do know that Chasity was bailed out a few hours ago," she replied.

"Well that's a good start, now we got to get Lil John John and Neko out next," Rashad replied. Shaking her head, all she could do was regret calling her son, asking him to come check on his little sister whom been attacked by their next door neighbors.

"Son, are you mad at me?"

Glancing at his mom after asking the question, Rashad couldn't believe his ears. She was feeling just as guilty as her son for putting him and his friends in such a situation. Answering the question from the bottom of his heart, "You can never make me mad, ma. We all we got. If you rewind ime and tell me someone attacked Aleysia, I'll take that same ride again, even if it's by myself."

Replying with just a smile let Rashad know that he had lifted her spirit, which was his goal.

Although his spirits were low due to the fact that his friends were still incarcerated, the last thing he wanted was to pass that energy off to the next. Rashad's mother, Ms. Tara was financially unstable to contribute as much as she wanted to, but everyone had her full support outside of that. These last two days had been rough for Rashad mentally and the wounds on his body made it no better physically. After spending a few days sleeping on a two-inch thick mattress that lay on a metal bunkbed, the queen size pillow top bed was calling his name. Arriving in front of Grandma Betty's home, it wasn't much to say and before closing the passenger side door, Ms. Tara last words are, "I love you son. Get you some rest and try not to think so much. Call me when you get up." Ending the conversation with an "I love you," the next thing on Rashad's mind was to call and check on Chasity. Placing a call from his cell phone, she answers on the final ring.

"What's up." From the tone of those two words, Rashad realized Chasity wasn't in the mood to talk.

"Are you okay?" Rashad asked.

"Yea, I'm good," said Chasity.

"Why you so dry? What's wrong? Talk to me," Rashad said as he pleads for Chasity to communicate.

"Because man you just don't understand. A male police officer sexually harassed me, feeling on my vagina and I couldn't even stop him," Chasity calmly explained.

"What?!" screamed Rashad, "Did you get his name?!"

"Yes, I told my dad and he's handling it. When I came out that back room from dressing into that jumpsuit, it was a reason I looked at you like that. We were told to squat down for the officers to make sure we weren't smuggling anything through our private areas. The girl next to me was on her period and as we squatted down, her period blood splattered all over my feet! Shit was disgusting and that's what made me tell you to get me out of here."

"Damn bay, I'm so sorry you had to go through that," Rashad said genuinely. "Yea, it's cool. I need some time to myself though, Rashad. These last few days had been overbearing for me and I hope you can understand that."

Although he wanted to see Chasity face to face, Rashad had no choice but to understand her reason for wanting space and respected her request by cutting the conversation short. Once one problem was solved, another equation presented itself and although Rashad wanted to solve them all, he didn't have the answers.

Chapter 19. *The County Of Clayton*

It's been two weeks since Neko and Lil John John have been incarcerated. Despite the fact that Rashad kept in touch with both of their mothers, he had yet to communicate with either friends. They both had a bond that could be paid but due to financial issues, they had to wait out the storm to see if there's a way to be released without spending unnecessary money. As Rashad sat in his comfortable rocking chair given to him by family after being released from Grady, the call he'd been waiting 2 weeks for finally comes through. It was Mrs. Whitfield, Lil John John's mother calling with Lil John John on three-way.

"Fool!" Lil John John said excitedly.

"My boy!!! How you doing bro?" Rashad asked.

"I'm good fool. How you doing nigga? You the one caught the worst end of the stick," Lil John John said.

"Man I'm sorry bro. I'm sorry for putting y'all niggas through this shit. Made me feel like I should've just went by myself," Rashad responded.

"Nigga you talking crazy, if we had to go down there and do this shit all over again that's what we gone do. You my nigga fool, don't ever forget that," said Lil John John.

"So what's up with the bond what y'all need?" Rashad asked curiously.

"I'm straight fool, mom's got me a lawyer already so Ima just ride it out. Ain tryna spend no unnecessary money just to go down anyway. Just check on mom for me to see if she need anything."

"I got ya bro. Stay down for me, all this shit gone be over soon," Rashad said.

"I already know it, just take care of your body nigga and stay on top of your health," Lil John John said.

The conversation put a smile on Rashad's face for the first time in two weeks. Since being incarcerated, he'd had his mind on his friends more than he did on his own recovery but the conversation he just had with Lil John John sure took a few pounds off his shoulders. Not long after that convo did Neko reach out to Rashad through a mutual female friend using three-way. Excited to hear from Neko, Rashad was prepared to hear positivity but got caught with a rude awakening.

"What's going on bro? How you doing?" Rashad asked.

"Shid you tell me. I hear ya girl all at the mall getting her nails done and shit but ain't nobody got nothing on my bond. What the fuck going on out there?" asked Neko.

Rashad was caught completely off guard. Growing up, Neko and Rashad's relationship was much more closer than the one of Rashad and Lil John John's but it seemed as when shit got real, it became obvious no one had his back the way Lil John John did.

"Bro you serious right now? You ain't talking right, I need you to stay down for me, this shit gone be over soon." Rashad said as he urged Neko to calm down.

"Man I always stay down and look where that shit got me. I got kids nigga, you don't have no kids, so you can't feel where I'm coming from," Neko replied.

Two weeks in and it felt like his best friend growing up was turning on him. The happiness Lil John John gave Rashad a few hours ago had been aken away just that fast. The hopes that Rashad had for his friends not kicking him while he's already down had left his body as he sat on the front porch listening to Neko complain about everything he already felt guilty about. Hanging up the phone in Rashad's face, he remained seated on the front porch as he dwelled on all the problems he had no control of. Remembering that he had $100 bill in his pocket, which was all he had to his name, Rashad headed to the store to get change. From the store he walks to Allen Temple while bloods seeks through his gauze where Neko's mother resides and gives her half of what's in his pocket to put towards anything concerning Neko. Leaving Allen Temple, the next destination was Lil John John's home, and after offering the very last $50 bill to his name, Mrs. Whitfield, Lil John John's mom insisted that Rashad keep his money because she had everything taken care of. The only thing she asked for from Rashad was his prayers but whether she asked or not Lil John John was going to receive those anyway. Arriving back to Grandma Betty's home to regroup, Rashad wanted to be around some love so of course he calls the one person he always turns to. Appearing close to sunset was Chasity, in her mother's 4-door black Infiniti sedan as she watched Rashad walk out the front door. As he opens the car door, he places his 38. Revolver special on the floor next to his right foot, which he deeply regrets later.

The plans were to go catch a movie but due to the couple's frisky and freakiness, plans seem to change unexpectedly a lot. Now that the plans to the movies were cancelled, the two decided to head back to Chasity's mom's house and after entering the home, Rashad instantly regretted calling her for what he figured would be great vibes to enjoy. After lying on her bed, Chasity reached for a Xanax pill and bottle of blue dot Cîroc. Expecting the pill to be for Chasity, she tried stuffing it in Rashad's mouth as he resisted.

"Chasity, chill… Haven't been out the hospital a whole month yet. I don't need that," Rashad said.

"I got you baby. This Xanax and liquor is not bad for you. If anything, it should help you sleep better," Chasity said with confidence. Rashad was no stranger to drugs and actually had no problem with Chastity doing them, it was the fact knowing that Rashad body was at his lowest point internally and common sense should have made her realize that polluting his body with drugs would do everything but help him. Going against his first mind, Rashad eventually puts his guard down and was asleep from the mixture twenty minutes later.

1:00 in the afternoon, Rashad wakes up restless as if he hasn't received any sleep, which was a sign the Xanax was still on his back. He was becoming fed up with the care Chasity had for his health and he started to realize he would never grow mentally as long as she's around. It wasn't the first time and he was sure it wouldn't be the last of her careless actions. As these thoughts roamed through his head, he also realized this was the same girl that took it upon herself to wipe his ass in that hospital when he couldn't so it wasn't easy as 1,2,3 but it was time for a change.

Remembering he left his 38. Revolver special in her mother's car, he told Chasity to remind her mom to put the gun up in a safe place. His goal was to get up early enough to get it out the car before she headed to work but that Xanax had other plans. To his surprise, Chasity's mother let her mechanic take the gun, convincing her that he had put it in her car during a car inspection. Rashad couldn't believe it, hoping it was a joke but being nothing other than serious.

As much as he loved Chasity with everything in him, the energy that came with being around her could no longer be ignored and all the signs were telling him to give up. Rashad was ready to go home, but had no ride so he had to wait on Chasity's mother to return home from work, without his gun of course. A few hours later coming down the driveway was Chasity's mom as Rashad stands at the front door insinuating his impatience for wanting to go home. Heading to Adamsville to drop Rashad off, the ride was more awkward than ever.

"So who gone pay for my 38?" Rashad asked.

"What you mean? That's your fault. Didn't nobody tell you to leave that gun in my mama car. That's on you. You can't be a boss till you take a loss," said Chasity.

Rashad's instincts wanted to bash her head through the driver side window, but he who angers you only controls you so Rashad played it off the best way he knew how, remaining silent. Not caring for anything Rashad experienced this morning, Chasity arrived in front of Grandma Betty's home where they parted ways without even speaking. Although they had their many differences in the past, there was something about this moment that really stuck with Rashad which caused him to officially wash his hands.

In spite of the fact that Rashad was more active than he was a few weeks ago, his body continued to ache every other hour as he tried to stay off his feet as much as possible. Sleeping the remainder of the day away after such a tough morning, Rashad was awoken by a knock at his window at 6 a.m. the next morning. He slid the curtains slightly open to see a toothpick body covered in clothes. It was Lil John John and he had finally been released after three weeks. Opening the front door to let him in, it registered that Rashad's home was the first stop Lil John John made after being released and also made it known that Neko had been released as well. God is good and Rashad couldn't thank him enough. Despite the fact the group of friends had overcome a storm, they still have one last battle, proving to the judge that they were innocent.

Chapter 20. *Pressure Burst Pipes But It Also Creates Diamonds*

It had been eight months since Rashad had left the hospital. His body was healing slowly but surely physically and mentally. Lil John John had both casts taken off each arm but had yet to gain full control of either wrist. Neko's scars were all healed but he continued to sometimes have pain beneath the skin. Although Chasity and Rashad weren't on the best of terms, it was also understood that the wounds she suffered on her neck healed as expected as well.

The friends had been called to Clayton County courtroom at least four times before being forced to reschedule due to lack of evidence, communication, and numerous other things. The County of Clayton was trying to railroad the young boys from Atlanta, but the devil is a liar. In the meantime, a mutual friend, an up and coming comedian who went by the name FatAndPaid, influenced Lil John John. His name was self-explanatory and he insisted that Lil John John begin making comedy videos for Instagram, which he had a natural talent for making people laugh. Thinking nothing of it, Lil John John didn't even have a camera phone. Forcing the idea on Lil John John every chance he gets, FatAndPaid's idea eventually influenced him to steal his first iPhone. The attention that Lil John John began to receive was much more than anyone expected. The videos shifted his campaign to become so large that he landed a movie role with A+ actors such as Danny Glover! He also caught other celebrities' attention such as Nick Cannon who blessed him with a role on MTV's own WildNOut, which he elevated for the world to know him as DC Young Fly.

Of course the devil was working but God was working 100 times harder and faster. Rashad eventually began searching for his next girlfriend, which brought him in contact with his high school crush, Lashae. Lashae was his breath of fresh air and everything he needed to keep his mind off negativity as he grew into the man he always knew he was capable of being. The couple also gave birth to a handsome son by the name of 'Shyne Karson Thomas' born Aug 2, 2017 at Emory Hospital, the same hospital that gave birth to his father. The birth of his son gave Rashad so much happiness because he remembers being told in Grady hospital that if he makes it alive, he will be brain dead for sure. Not only did Rashad beat death but he also mastered the technique of walking by faith not by sight and doing everything the doctors said he couldn't. Neko continued being the best father to his four kids and regardless of the misunderstanding he and Rashad had while incarcerated, their relationship is still going strong as brothers. Neko also helps run a non-profit organization by the name of "Sell Hope Not Dope" aimed for kids with dreams, which is also growing bigger day by day.

A few weeks passed by before Da Crew as well as Chasity were called back into the Clayton County courtroom. The energy was different as it was made clear that there would be no rescheduling this time. There was somewhat nervous energy passed on through the group of friends because the judge that was appointed to their case had a reputation for sending her own son to prison. Everyone had a lawyer except Rashad, but he was just as confident. Lil John John, Neko, and Chasity all plead guilty to every charge except child cruelty. Rashad tried his best to convince his friends that there's no way that either of them committed a crime, but it was apparent he had to take his own shot.

"Mr. Thomas, are you sure you want to take this to trial?" the public defender asked.

"Yes," Rashad replied.

The Caucasian redhead public defender walked inside the courtroom, which she stayed in for ten minutes as Rashad, Ms. Tara, his youngest brother Jake, and little sister Aleysia stood in the hallway. The public defender exited the courtroom to approach Rashad for the second time hoping he was nervous enough to change his mind.

"Mr. Thomas are you positive you want to take this to trial?"

Looking confused, Rashad begins to think she's deaf.

"Did you not hear my son tell you we're taking it to trial?" Ms. Tara said.

"Yes mam, I understand that but your words don't matter, it's only up to your son," the public defender said.

"And I said I'm taking it to trial loud and clear! What part of that don't you understand? Rashad asked.

It was almost crystal clear that the public defender was attempting to convince Rashad to throw his life away. After turning around to head back into the courtroom, five minutes later she returns in the hallway with a frown on her face as she said, "Mr. Thomas, your case has been officially dismissed."

"Thank you Jesus!" yelled Ms. Tara. Since staying at the courthouse to hear Rashad's verdict, Neko was stuck with a confused look on his face showing regret for pleading guilty to his charges. Rashad tried his best to convince his friends not to give in but apparently everyone had different fears. Rashad was extremely grateful for his blessings and now that he got that monkey off his back it was time for a celebration. The celebration included going to Club Mansion with Lashae by his side. Being that he didn't club often he was determined to make the best out of this night because he deserved it. Leaving the club, Rashad received a call in the midst of driving, which stuck with him years after. Lil Kirk had been murdered while at a music studio. It hurt Rashad so bad that he couldn't even hold the tears back from crying in front of Lashae, which forced him to pull over on the side of the road and regroup. All he could remember was Lil Kirk saying, "These streets don't love nobody my boy, go to school!"

The following day Rashad enrolled into Atlanta State Metro College where he elevated his thoughts, which allowed him to create *Scars Of Wisdom*.

To my readers,

If you asked me a year ago if I were to ever write a book, I would probably look confused but so many things can happen within 365 days. Life taught me that you miss 100% of the shots that you DO NOT take so I hope I encourage you to take yours. Impossible spells I'm possible, so as long as God wakes me up everyday I will be determined to make tomorrow better than yesterday. I'm very thankful for all of my supporters as well as my haters, you're all highly appreciated!!!!!!!!

Rest In Peace,

> Anthony 'Lil Kirk' Hill
>
> Katerius 'Richie' Moody
>
> Charlotte Wright
>
> Betty Jean Thomas
>
> Marvin Wallace Jr
>
> Marvin Wallace Sr
>
> Karen 'Denise' Wright
>
> Jesse 'Buster' Wright
>
> Tillie Mae Wright
>
> Jesse 'Lou' Jernigan
>
> Renardo 'Nardo' Varner
>
> Adam 'Peanut Da Don' Williams
>
> Obadiah Chibuike Njoki
>
> Jonathon Benn
>
> Brenda Monfort
>
> Shanequa Sullivan
>
> And every other beautiful soul I may have forgotten.

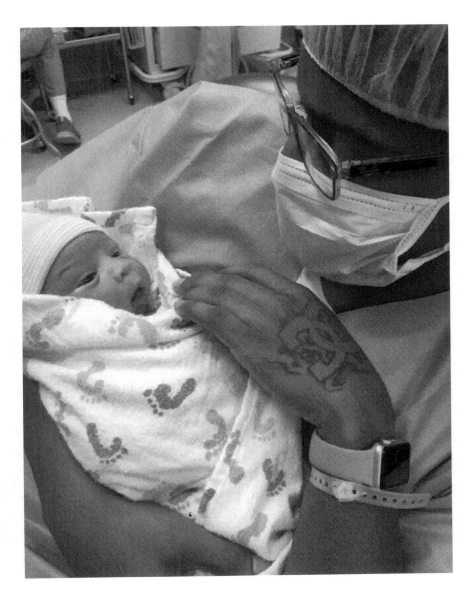

'Shyne Karson Thomas'

Born August 2, 2017 at 2:08 P.M.

Rashad, Neko, and Lil John John at Clayton County Superior Court.

Rashad & Lil John John on Rashad's final day inside Grady Hospital.

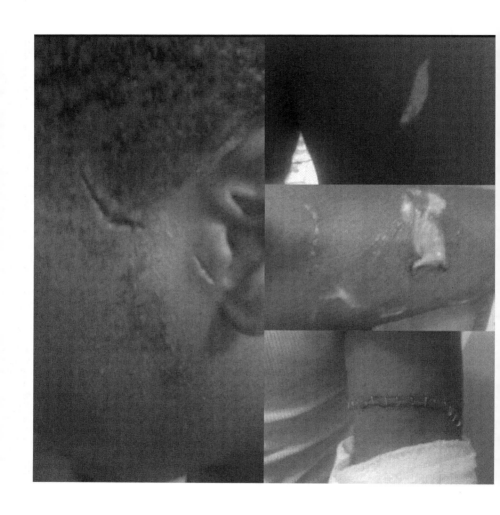

Neko & The War Wounds He Suffered

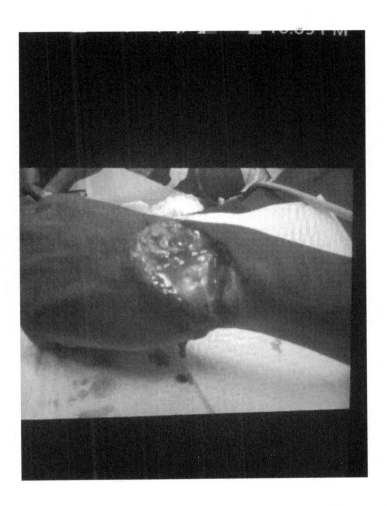

A photo of Lil John John's right wrist after the altercation in Clayton County

Rashad & baby sister Aleysia a few years after his hospital visit.

The 1ˢᵗ photo Rashad took of himself after waking up from ICU

Rashad and Lil John John after a sold out show in the hometown at The Fox Theatre.

A photo of Rashad and Neko together on a hot summer day

A captured photo of Lil John John and Rashad after having a glorious day in the dice game

Lil Kirk alongside Rashad at Crim High School Graduation Ceremony 2011'

Rashad & Uncle KennyMan

(R.I.P Simpson Road "Pudge")

Lil John John A.K.A. DC Young Fly entertaining his fans with his God given talent at a sold out show in Columbia, South Carolina

Rashad alongside his father and mother after his Crim High School
graduation ceremony 2011'

Product Of Environment…

Made in the USA
Columbia, SC
25 August 2020

17616805R00072